INNER STRENGTH INNER PEACE II

More Life-Changing Lessons From the World's Greatest

Tim McClellan

Budo Inc.

Library of Congress Cataloging - in - Publications Data.
McClellan, Tim
Inner Strength Inner Peace II: More Life-Changing Lessons From the World's Greatest

Budo Incorporated
2815 E. Libra Street
Gilbert, AZ 85234

Cover photo acknowledgements:
Crystal Rezzonico (Photo by Deena Glaab)
Rosie (Photo by Tim McClellan)
Koco Garcia (Photo courtesy Koco Garcia)
Jeff Dodge (Photo by Yoko Ishida)
Jim Cope (Photo courtesy Brittney Cope)
Pat Misch (Photo by Phil Konort)
Charley Martin (Photo courtesy Charley Martin)

www.StrengthAndPeace.com

DEDICATION
To FIGHTERS!

I love fighters. I love all kinds of fighters. I thoroughly respect fighters. I am proud to have braved many challenges and infirmities as a fighter.

To date, I have fought—in one combative system or another—many of the world's greatest. Kevin Jackson, Mark Kerr, Mark Coleman and Dan Severn were all top-ranked mixed martial artists in the world at one point in their careers. Jackson and Kenny Monday won Olympic Gold Medalists in wrestling. Super heavyweight Angelo Parisi earned the Olympic gold in judo. Christophe and Brian Leininger were national champions in judo. Melvin Douglas won a World Champion in wrestling. Hiroshi Allen won three World Championships in karate and 17 National Championships. Cardo Urso attained the black belt rank in fourteen different disciplines. I fought them all, and many more beasts like National Karate Champions Jeff Dodge, Simeon Ekrissin, Kyle Harder and Jihone Du. I love them all.

Although there is no doubt that I have benefited greatly from doing combat with these talented athletes, with all due respect, they're not the fighters I admire most. I am dedicating this book to those who are fighting for more than athletic conquest. This book is dedicated to two close friends and heroes of mine that are fighting for their very lives.

Dr. Judd Biasiotto was one of the first sports psychologists ever to be hired by a professional team. He graduated from the University of Notre Dame and has written over 50 books and 600 magazine articles. He squatted more weight than any drug-free powerlifter in his weight class in the world. He then went on to be the oldest ever Mr. American in bodybuilding. I wrote a chapter about him in my first book *Inner Strength Inner Peace*. He has been a tenured professor, a sculptor and basically anything else he ever wanted to be in life. Simply said, there isn't anything Dr. Judd cannot do. There never has been. He is like a real-life Superman in that sense and is literally a hero and

role model to me. He is also currently one of only 50 people in this world suffering from both Multiple Sclerosis and Muscular Dystrophy simultaneously. For a man who was the strongest of the strong, the smartest of the smart and could do anything in the world he wanted, it just doesn't seem fair. Yet whenever I talk to him, even though he suffers severe pain, he tells me he loves me and asks me if there is anything he can do for *me*. That's what a real man does. He thinks of others first and acts upon it. I strive everyday to be more like Judd, knowing full well I could never be him. I just want to be closer. He shines as an example for all of us.

Todd VanBodegom-Smith was my college teammate in powerlifting. He was an All-American at East Stroudsburg State College. I wrote a chapter about him in my first book. Todd suffers from amyotrophic lateral sclerosis (ALS), often referred to as Lou Gehrig's disease. He no longer weighs a rock-hard 165 pounds, and he no longer routinely squats over 500 pounds. Today, he sits in a wheelchair, unable to stand up, and he only weighs 85 pounds. It has been said that those with ALS live their lives locked in a prison. Todd's mind is as sharp as ever, but his body is paralyzed. I imagine it is like being locked in a cage. When I visit Todd in Pennsylvania, I see death in his body but life in his eyes. He's still the incredible, lovable, smart, caring guy with an unparalleled personality. Because of the lessons I've learned from Judd, I tell Todd that I love him and always ask what I can do to help him.

The competitive fighting I do for sport pales in comparison. These guys are the true heroes, the real fighters. May they continue to fight the good fight, and win. May they both know that I love them. There are no finer human beings. I am eternally grateful for the ways that both of them have taught me to become a better man.

EDITOR'S NOTE: *Since the initial writing of this dedication Todd VanBodegom-Smith finally lost his eleven-year battle against ALS. May you rest in eternal glory, Todd.*

ACKNOWLEDGMENTS

SAMANTHA WEISS - EDITOR

Words cannot express how much I appreciate Samantha's work in editing both *Inner Strength, Inner Peace* and this book. Samantha is a graduate of MIT with a B.S. in chemical engineering, and another in writing. She currently is working towards her Ph.D. in computational fluid dynamics at the University of Illinois/Champaign.

YAWNA ALLEN - COPY EDITOR

I have had the privilege of training Yawna throughout the early stages of her professional tennis career. Yawna graduated with a B.A. in news-editorial journalism from Oklahoma State University, where she starred on the Cowgirls tennis team. Her willingness to help and expertise are as vast as her smile.

KRISTLE SCHULZ - EDITOR/FORMATTING

Kristle is another athlete I have had the privilege of training. She was a standout student and volleyball player at Xavier College Preparatory in Phoenix, Arizona and now is working towards her Bachelors degree at the University of Arizona. Her computer skills, patience and work ethic were a tremendous asset to this project.

COURTNEY EKMARK - WEB DESIGN

Watching Courtney Ekmark grow and helping her pursue her dreams of becoming a top-notch collegiate basketball player has been a blessing in my life. I appreciate her help and support in designing the web site for this book as well as for *Inner Strength, Inner Peace*.

JULIA VANHELDER - COVER DESIGNER

I have seen Julia grow from an eight-year-old with crooked bangs in the judo dojo, to a professional young woman. Her hard work and creativity in designing the covers shows her immense talent. Julia can be reached at judosuperstar@gmail.com.

CONTENTS

INTRODUCTION

The response I received from *Inner Strength, Inner Peace* was truly heartwarming. In that book, I wrote that I felt that I've been blessed in my life to meet so many remarkable people. That has not changed. Not a day goes by that I don't feel blessed by those folks, and so many of the new ones I get to interact with.

It is my hope that the stories in this book will help you recognize the blessings in your life and receive them with gratitude.

Chapter 1

INTENTION

AENEAS WILLIAMS

"Do you not know that in a race all the runners run, but only one gets the prize? Run in such a way as to get the prize. Everyone who competes in the games goes into strict training. They do it to get a crown that will not last; but we do it to get a crown that will last forever. Therefore I do not run like a man running aimlessly; I do not fight like a man beating the air. No, I beat my body and make it my slave so that after I have preached to others, I myself will not be disqualified for the prize."

-1 Corinthians 9: 24-27

I will never forget the time I spent training Aeneas Williams and the lesson of intention I learned by observing his actions.

A decade ago I received a call from Williams, who, at the time, was arguably the top cornerback in all of football. He asked me if we could set up a meeting to talk about training options during the off-season. I have been through these meetings hundreds of times with professional and world-class athletes. They are basically all the same. It's fun to get to meet someone new, to find out what the keys have been to their successes, and to provide council on how I might contribute to their future performance. The athletes typically ask me two questions, perhaps three to four tops.

This was not the case with Aeneas Williams. When he first came in the door, I sensed that here was a man of character and humility. But he quickly got to work, grilling me with an intention that seemed as if he was interviewing me for the position of President of the United States. I think he might have asked me forty questions that day. I soon found that he approaches everything in life that same way.

Our running sessions that summer started at nine each morning. The day never came that Aeneas wasn't there by eight-fifteen. He would stretch as if he was trying to be the best at the world at it. He would put himself through a thorough warm-up by himself before the other pros would arrive at the facility. Then there were the prayers. An ordained minister, Aeneas would lead the Christian athletes in the group through long, strong, purposeful prayers. It was an awesome sight to see his devotion. By eight-fifty he would be standing on the goal line ready to work, fully prepared and anxious to lead the drills. Aeneas was our natural choice to be the first guy in line to set the tempo for each drill. The leader sets the tone for the whole group and a strong leader can bring an entire group up to another level. I can't imagine anyone ever doing it better than Aeneas Williams. When we asked him to run ten yards he never ran less than thirty. If we asked him to run fifty he would run eighty. He worked this way through every drill, every day, every week, every month. We demanded a lot of him, and he demanded a lot of himself. This is the honest-to-God truth. I actually saw him run through a twenty-foot long speed and agility ladder and run an extra eighty yards on his own after completing the drill.

Our run groups consisted most days of twenty to thirty N.F.L. players representing several N.F.L. teams. As the tempo setter of our group, Aeneas demanded this work ethic of everyone, including opposing team players that he would have to directly cover during the upcoming season. Every time we had long, hard runs that would test not only their physical ability but also their mental toughness, he would line up directly beside Philadelphia Eagles' wide receiver Charles Johnson. Williams knew full well he would be covering Charles all game long in two games in the upcoming season, since the Cardinals played the Eagles twice. He knew Charles was a training animal, and he knew Charles was a great wide receiver. He also knew the better he helped Charles to become, the better he himself would have to be. This was Aeneas Williams' intention.

After one session, he came to me with questions about my experiences with martial arts. He asked me if I would help him with some striking movements with his hands; a skill he felt would allow him to jam receivers on the playing field. One Saturday morning at my home dojo, we worked from eight to nine and as usual, Aeneas gave me everything he had. At that time, a group of judo and Brazilian ju-jitsu fighters came in for our training session. As my session with Aeneas had ended, I immersed myself in the fighting. A good hour later I realized that Aeneas sat at the edge of the mat, staring with intensity, as though absorbing everything around him. He was also chatting with my wife Janet, a high-ranking brown belt in judo at the time. What a kind man, I thought -- a tightly scheduled NFL player taking time out to chat with my wife.

Later, I found that Aeneas wasn't being merely courteous; he was picking Janet's brain, trying to relate the judo techniques he had just watched to the game of football. Receivers often grabbed his jersey toward the end of a play to prevent him from assisting in more tackles. He thought if he learned to break their grip, a technique he saw in judo, he could get more assists.

This isn't to say he wasn't courteous, by any means. He was kind to

5

every one he met. With that distinct civility of a southern gentleman, he even called my wife Miss Janet. He graciously signed autographs for any kid who asked, and took the time to make each feel important. He did everything with intention.

Former star receiver Frank Sanders once pointed out an interesting characteristic about Aeneas that we didn't see—his ability to relax, when appropriate. As Frank said, "Tim, Aeneas out-trains everyone in the game, but if you notice, he seems to work real hard for five weeks and then he'll take the sixth week off and go to the Bahamas and relax for a week. He works exceptionally hard and he rests exceptionally hard as well." So this became my observation—Frank was right. Aeneas would outwork everyone and then he would get away from it all, he would also out-rest everyone, pulling over for a personal "pit stop" to recharge everything, so that he could hit it hard again.

Working with and observing Aeneas Williams was a great privilege. He is a great man and was a great player. He did everything with intention. He prayed with intention. He played with intention. He befriended with intention. He helped with intention. Aeneas Williams is one of those rare individuals you are fortunate to meet once in a lifetime. I hope he knows that the lesson of intention I learned by observing his actions will never be forgotten. His light shines by example. Aeneas never had to say a word; we all knew why he ran -- to win the prize.

Today Williams is retired from professional football. He is now Pastor Aeneas of The Spirit Church in St. Louis. Pastor Aeneas is no different than player Aeneas. I attended service there just this morning on a business trip. It brought a smile to see the service start precisely at nine and to see Pastor Aeneas with unmistakable intention in sharing God's word. I left knowing without doubt Pastor Aeneas will indeed get that prize. It could be no other way. Thank you player Aeneas. God bless you Pastor Aeneas. I will proceed with intention.

▲

Chapter 2

COURAGE

SENSEI GARY VENEROSO

"God helps the brave."
    -Johann von Schiller, *Wilhelm Tell*

Sensei Gary Veneroso grew up in a small, blue-collar Pennsylvania town. Life there has always been about work. For some, this means getting up in the dark of night to work twelve-hour days of grueling physical labor. These folks come home exhausted almost every day. Sensei Gary epitomizes that kind of work ethic. He owns a small independent gym in Hazleton, Pennsylvania, called Ultimate Fitness. There, he works tirelessly to provide for the people of his town. You won't find forty brand-new, expensive Woodway treadmills there, like you might find in the high-end fitness chains in Phoenix. You also won't find the latest high-tech machines. But you'll find one good man, using the resources that he's got, helping lots of people to lead healthier lives.

When I met him in 1993, I told Gary that I was a student of Wado-ryu karate. At that time, Gary already owned his gym and was a lifetime martial artist who had developed the ability to teach courage. He gave me the confidence and direction to break a pine board, then two, then three and then seven. Pine led to cinder. Cinder led to competitive breaking tournaments. Somewhere along the way I found myself lying on a bed of nails while stacks of cinder blocks were placed on my chest and smashed with a sledgehammer. This led to walking on broken glass, kneeling on the glass and having blocks on my forearm broken with a sledgehammer. Against my poor mother's will, I submitted myself to having blocks broken over the back of my head with a sledgehammer while I had a razor sharp katana (samurai sword) firmly imbedded in front of my neck. Sensei Gary asked me to face many fears. He also taught me, "face the fear and the fear disappears." And as he promised, they are no longer fears. The fears have disappeared. More important, I've learned to incorporate the philosophy into my daily life.

I wasn't born with unusual courage. I have that now because I had a great teacher. I wish the whole world could have prolonged exposure to Sensei Gary Veneroso.

Chapter 3

INTENSITY

SIMEON RICE

"I have always demanded a great deal from myself. Those who would demand equally of themselves, I think would find little difficult in working with me. Those who demand less of themselves might find it extremely difficult."
    -Unknown

At one of Simeon's intense workouts: champion boxer Junior Butler and myself with Simeon.

I wish I could include a video clip of Simeon Rice in this chapter, or at least one of those interactive Harry Potter photographs. I would love for everyone to see the side of Simeon that I see. I coached Simeon in his off-season workouts for over six years. I always have loved working with athletes who have ascended to the top of their game and Simeon did just that. In his prime he rushed the passer as well as anybody ever has in the game of football. I can only describe Simeon's off-season thought process, philosophy and work ethic as intense, but that would be selling him short. Even ultra-intense doesn't do him justice. I would need that video clip to convey intensity that can't be conveyed any other way. That is Simeon Rice.

When I met him, I thought he was flat-out crazy. I interviewed him thoroughly, as a good strength and conditioning coach should. When we finished talking, I felt compelled to see if I had heard him accurately.

"Sim, you're telling me you go out and run ten timed two-hundred meter runs with the track coach at Arizona State University. You then go through a complete boxing workout with former world contender Junior Butler. You finish by sparring several rounds with Butler before you play basketball. You then want to come to me to lift weights. Is this correct?"

"Yeah."

That was it. That's how Simeon Rice saw things. He had to run as part of his living, so he wanted to run more than anyone else in the game. He had to knock down the hands of offensive lineman who were trying to pass block him, so he wanted to have the fastest hands in the game. He knew Junior Butler would put him through sessions as intense as anyone. Simeon also knew he needed to accelerate, decelerate, change direction and jump like an NBA player at times, so he played a lot of basketball. Most times, he played with NBA players during their off-season. He understood that the brutality of football demands an ultra-strong body. He therefore demanded that we train like animals in the weight room.

After years of studying this, I benefited tremendously from my exposure to Simeon's intensity. What's good for the goose is good for the gander. Simeon wanted his workouts intense and I made them ultra-intense. But I've always known in my heart I had to do the same in my own workouts. I'd be living a lie if I talked up the need to do such workouts and fell short when my turn came to stand up and take the medicine. In that way, Simeon Rice has helped me immeasurably to become a better athlete.

I wish I had stories about Simeon Rice that are cute, funny or at least intriguing. I do not. This may sound odd, especially after so many years; we didn't talk much during the workouts. I never knew how he was, how his weekend was, or what he had planned for the upcoming holiday. It was all about business. He was intense, I was intense and the machine fed itself. When we did talk, we usually spoke about intense things, like the philosophies of Genghis Khan, Julius Caesar, Alexander the Great or some other intense leader. I assure you, the subject of Harry Potter never came up.

Simeon: a newspaper story I read claimed that Genghis Khan's DNA has been traced to over twenty thousand descendants. I'd be willing to bet you are one of them. Whether you are playing basketball like an NBA guy, sparring with a world contender, running like an Olympic track athlete, writing your screenplay, manufacturing your T3K clothing line, or cranking up the heat in our gym, I hope you never lose your intensity. That is a gift both to me and to the other athletes who are fortunate enough to take notice.

Chapter 4

▲

BEATING THE ODDS
TOM POTI

"A part of control is learning to correct your weaknesses. The person doesn't live who was born with everything. Sometimes he has one weak point; generally he has several. The first thing is to know your faults and then take on a systematic plan of correcting them. You know the old saying about a chain being only as strong as its weakest link. The same can be said in the chain of skills a man forges."

-Babe Ruth

Tom (on left) with Dan LaCouture.

Tom Poti is a former National Hockey League (NHL) All-Star player who has had a long, illustrious career. He was on the 1998-1999 All-Rookie Team as a member of the Edmonton Oilers. He was an integral member of the 2002 Olympic team, which won a silver medal. I had the pleasure of meeting Tom years ago, when I helped to train him in the summer before his rookie season.

Tom is living proof some athletes can excel despite their genes. Tom has a genetic blueprint that would keep most anyone from athletic accomplishments. He had gone into Boston University as an unusually talented hockey player, one of the very few who excelled as both a front line offense player and a back line defender. In a few years, he declared himself eligible for the NHL draft and expected to be a first round pick. That never happened. At the time, Tom was a severe asthmatic and so his stock plummeted. He was picked in the third round, which cost him a great deal of money. His asthma was so bad during the summer I worked with him that he could not run outside at all. For some unknown reason he could get away with running on treadmills indoors, but even that presented a challenge on some days. The asthma, as horrible and costly as it was, was only part of the battle Tom fought.

Tom Poti also suffers from severe food allergies, specifically peanuts, and just about every type of spice. Dan LaCouture, his college roommate and teammate for several years in the pros, tells stories about the lengths Tom has to go through just to receive nourishment.

A major television station once ran a feature documentary segment chronicling the time Dan almost accidentally killed Tom. According to Dan, the documentary was a national broadcast and flashed pictures of Dan when he was younger, had long hair, and was in the midst of an intense battle in a game. As Dan put it, "They showed this picture of me looking like a serial killer. Then they told the story of how I almost killed Tom.

"It was during college. I love peanut butter and jelly sandwiches, but I could never eat them around Tom because just the smell of peanut butter, even when unperceivable to us, could set off his allergy. I had to make these sandwiches at times when Tom wasn't around for many hours. Once Tom had left for class and wasn't scheduled to return for four hours. Half an hour after he left and I was sure he was in class and not coming back I made myself the peanut butter and jelly sandwich. My father called on the phone and I spoke to him briefly. This all ended about four hours before Tom was scheduled to return. As it turns out, Tom returned two hours later. I had just stepped out. When I returned a few minutes after he got back, he was slumped over on the bathroom floor. When I asked if he wanted me to call an ambulance he couldn't give me a verbal response. Had I known that would happen I would have never made that sandwich. I love Tommy and he's been a dear friend since we were fifteen. I had fans nationwide thinking I was some kind of bad guy."

Dan LaCouture (on left) and Tom, long reconciled since the peanut butter incident.

As if the peanut allergy weren't enough, Tom is so allergic to spices that his food options are limited. If he goes to a restaurant after a game looking for carbohydrates and protein, he has to go into the kitchen and ask the chef to cook his steak in a separate pan, freshly cleaned. The steak can only be cooked in water. Eating steak off a grill that had spices on it could put Tom back into the state Dan found him in. His food options include baked potatoes without condiments, plain rice, plain burgers and eggs. During the years Tom lived with Dan, the two used different George Foreman grills. Tom's was black and Dan's white; they could make no mistakes, or else the television stations might be back for a sequel.

During the three months I trained with him, Tom Poti was friendly, warm and caring. He never complained about the asthma or the severity of it. He never complained about his food allergies or how difficult simply nourishing his body was. Most of all, he never complained about trying to be an elite athlete in spite of these atypical hardships. That summer, Tom Poti showed me how a person with an extraordinary attitude can beat extraordinary odds.

Chapter 5

▲

WILL

CRYSTAL REZZONICO

"Keep your dreams alive. Understand to achieve anything requires faith and belief in yourself, vision, hard work, determination, and dedication. Remember all things are possible for those who believe."
-Gail Devers

I will never do this story justice. But because of her example of will, I have to try. I have to give my best.

Firefighter Crystal Rezzonico was out on a call. I would hate to say the words "routine call," because firefighters do things routinely, like risking their lives, entering burning buildings, witnessing death, seeing abuse and trying to make sense of extreme stupidity that most of us never do in our more comfortable lives. To call anything they do routine is to minimize bold and noble undertakings. Being a dedicated, caring, above-and-beyond person in everything she does, Rezzonico would have done a superb job on that call. She never got the chance.

It was on the way to that call that her fire truck was t-boned by a man driving at 68 miles per hour. Crystal was ejected from her seatbelt and out her door and flew sixty feet, landing head first onto the concrete of the median. Some years later, I met another firefighter, one who was called to her accident scene in the line of duty.

"There was so much blood, it was everywhere. She was lying facedown; limp as she could possibly be. I just knew she was dead," he later told me.

She did not die that day, even though that was expected. For weeks, some of the top specialists in Arizona counseled family members that any future looked dim for her. But Crystal's prognosis was eventually "upgraded" to a chance at a life of being fully incapacitated. The brilliant, exceptional firefighter with the strong will to live was apt to live life unable to walk, talk or even go to the bathroom by herself --not a life indeed for someone who had overachieved the previous forty-eight years on earth.

It was two years later my close friend and firefighter Linda Rider came into the gym and asked me for a favor. "Tim, would you please consider training a friend of mine – even though it might not be fit for your program."

"Linda, if you think your friend isn't a fit, he isn't. I don't do those."

"It's a woman. She's fifty years old and needs help with her balance. She lacks confidence in it," she replied.

This didn't help Linda's cause—yet she persisted. "Please. She's been in a terrible accident. She was supposed to die. She's a beautiful person and was a good athlete. She needs your help. She is like a 50-year old Jocelyn."

I had trained Jocelyn Brayer and loved it. She was a total package: fun, super athletic, hard working, appreciative and a knock-out. In one year, I trained her for a bodybuilding show (second place finisher) the pole vault (first place and record setter in the Police and Firefighter World Games) and for her wedding (hot bride).

How could a 50-year old accident-prone lady with little balance and little confidence be another Jocelyn? Very few of those exist.

I caved in. I did it for Linda. It was a favor. Her friend needed help. I respect our firefighters. Training them is special to me—its not just trying to put two more points on a score board—it's to help them save lives and to save their own.

I met Crystal that week and am thankful every day since then I did. It turns out this amazing firefighter, who normally saves lives had to have hers saved by someone else. That someone else was Dr. Jonathan Hott, a non-firefighter, who performed five surgeries on her brain. During one of those operations, Hott removed a quarter of her skull and froze it for weeks before he surgically placed it back.

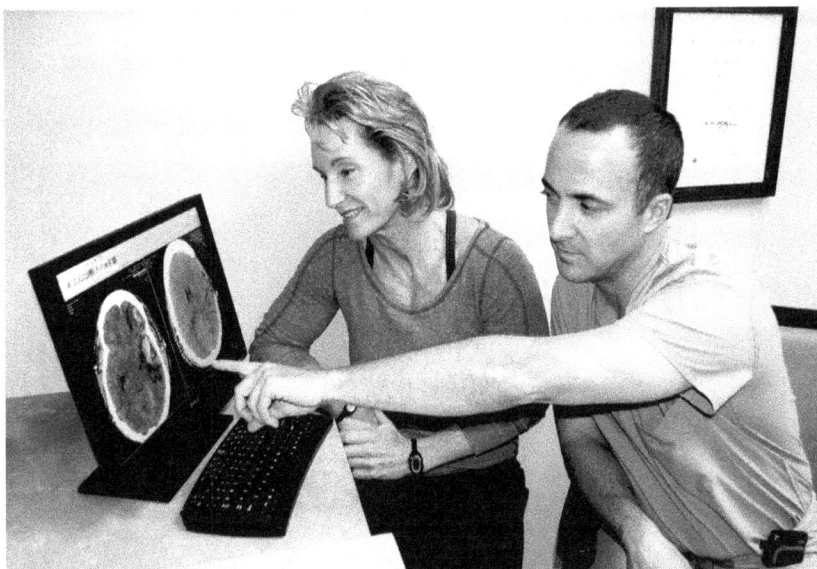

Crystal with Dr. Hott. The scan on the left is her skull post-injury. The one on the right is the revision minus the section of the skull they had to take out and freeze. (Photo courtesy John C. Lincoln Hospital.)

She spent two months in the hospital, and against all odds, she started to talk and walk. Twenty months later, against all predictions, she reported for duty once again as a firefighter. She was back in the truck.

Seeing this incredible, inspiring will first hand as I trained her, I had no choice to get out on the limb with her.

"Crystal, your body is responding so well to what we're doing. How would you feel about training for a real body building show?" Sometimes I go too far out on that limb.

Crystal Rezzonico went from perceived as dead to a sure bet to die, to an upgrade of an "incapacitated" prognosis to the 2011 Police and Firefighter

World Games Bodybuilding Champion!

Victor Frankl was an Austrian neurologist; a psychiatrist and holocaust victim who watched men die daily as prisoners of war. After studying these men, he said, "Everything can be taken from a man except his will."

So did Crystal Rezzonico.

Chapter 6

▲

ALL IN

JON READER

"Coach, I'm all in. All in!"
    -Jon Reader

I received a phone call from my dear friend Kevin Jackson in the spring of 2010. Kevin is someone special. At one time, he was the number one ranked mixed martial artist in the world. He was an Olympic Gold Medalist and twice a World Champion in freestyle wrestling. Believe it or not, he was also the U.S. Olympic team coach. Imagine taking three endeavors to the highest level worldwide. That's Kevin Jackson. He is both a man and a friend of that same highest caliber. There are none better, anywhere.

Kevin was the second year Head Wrestling Coach at his Alma matter, Iowa State University, a school that he had led to the National Championship as a wrestler decades earlier. He was asking for my help. He wanted me to provide guidance for one of the wrestlers he coached, Jon Reader. Jon had made All-American honors (placing in the top eight in the NCAA National Championships) both his freshman and sophomore years, but failed miserably in his junior year.

Apparently, Jon felt like he needed to get more out of his strength training workouts going into his senior season at ISU. He also had ambitions of moving to a heavier weight class, which is typically a kiss of death. After all, if you cannot finish in the top eight of your own class, how are you going to win one against bigger and stronger guys?

Admittedly, I wasn't initially pumped up about a wrestler with a declining outcome. On the other hand, this was a favor for Kevin Jackson and I love Kevin Jackson so I wrote a few programs over the next months and sent them on. A month or so later, I received a phone call from Kevin telling me Jon felt stronger on the mat when they wrestled. I took this as a good sign but honestly, I didn't know this Reader guy-- and feeling stronger is not a guarantee of winning wrestling matches.

Ultimately, I flew to Ames, Iowa to help out the entire ISU team. Apparently, Jon was a diligent worker, he was making appreciable gains and Coach Jackson saw an opportunity for other team members. I flew to Ames pretty much as a favor to the coach, as I didn't really know anyone, including Jon Reader.

Little did I know back then that I'd end up loving Ames, cherishing my role with the Iowa State wrestling program and that I'd fly there many more times over the next years.

What about Reader? How did all that play out?

Today he is on my short list. List of heroes, that is. He's there with Alexander the Great, Geronimo and Miyamoto Musashi.

My appreciation for Jon Reader grew throughout that season. It wasn't until I received an email from him three weeks prior to his Big 12 Conference Championships that I got to fully understand him, which led to my immense respect for his purpose. His email begins, "Coach McClellan, this is Jon Reader. My Big 12 Championships are in three weeks. I don't just want to win. I have to thoroughly dominate everyone there and throughout the NCAA National Championships. I feel like I am on track, but I need you to look over everything I am doing off-mat to make this the best it can be." He then proceeded to tell me every set, every exercise and every repetition he was doing in the weight room. That led to every bite of food he was eating and when he was doing so. I also found out his stretching and recuperation habits, sleep patterns and more. That was all I needed to know about Jon Reader. There is a huge difference between wanting to win and thoroughly dominating all of the top contenders in the country. I now knew him inside and out. In a nutshell, every cell of Jon Reader's body is geared towards winning wrestling matches and that is no over-exaggeration. He was "all in," every cell of his body. I've never seen anything like it in my thirty years of coaching. He is decidedly different. He's that one 100% focused athlete every coach dreams of coaching someday in their career, a human lion.

You better be ready if you're ever called to wrestle Jon Reader. There is no doubt he will be, and with the focus of a lion.

This is not to say this is a fairytale path he is on. First off, he trains way harder than others. I cannot picture any athlete out-working Jon Reader -- indeed a bold statement but a precise and sincere one.

He trains longer, harder and more often, but he also hurts more because of it. He uses up more mental energy off mat, a result of not turning his mind off between workouts. That alone makes many athletes weaken, but not Jon Reader. Then there's the ridicule for being the guy who stands out, who is so far outside the norm, who is alone on an island. The poor guy, he even told me one time his accomplished-athlete sister even calls him crazy. True to form, Jon Reader fights through the pain and ridicule. Every cell is focused towards winning, none towards criticism.

Jon Reader, despite going up a weight class, won the 2011 Big 12 Championships. He thoroughly dominated there, as per his focus. He followed that up by thoroughly dominating all opponents at the National Collegiate Championships. Bleeding profusely, his whole head taped up, Reader was invincible. He ended the season 39-0. It was the only way the season could have gone.

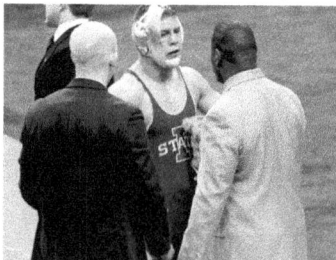

Jon, during the NCAA final, receiving instruction from Kevin Jackson, the best coach I have ever seen.

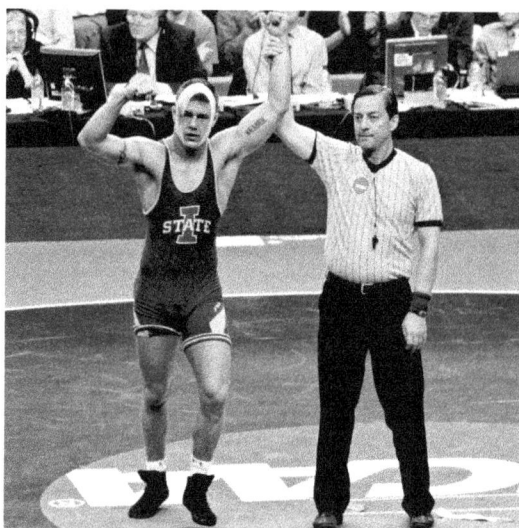

I love Jon Reader's ambition, his focus, determination, pain tolerance, work ethic and his passion. I sincerely wish everyone in the world were more like him, including myself. There are times when I receive a random text message from him, saying things like, "I'm seizing this day to its fullest," "I'm attacking today with an enthusiasm unknown to mankind," or "Victory is reserved for those willing to pay its price. Are you willing to pay its price?" I'm not sure why he sends me these at random times. I only know he is in my life for a purpose and I have to do the same. He's never been 99% of the way in, he's always 100% and I cannot give him anything less, not even 99%. This includes our midnight run on New Year's Eve 2012, where we bear-crawled up hills with a weighted sled in tow behind us.

I do feel bad about the poor guy being called crazy so much but truthfully, I have to ask: is he crazy or is he the sane one and everyone else is crazy? After all, he is a wonderful person, a strong Christian, a great friend and a devoted trainee. He has a close-knit family relationship and a beautiful girlfriend, Ashley. He's pursuing his dream of being the best in the world in the area of his passion. His support staff of coaches and training partners love him and go above and beyond for him. He is strong enough to take the path others won't and he has the self-satisfaction in his heart of having truly given 100%.

I think I just answered my previous question about which one is the sane one. Jon is. I love you Jon. Don't ever change. Stay "ALL IN."

Chapter 7

▲

ADAPTABILITY

BIG JIM TURPIN

"It's never too late to teach an old dog a new trick."
　　-Unknown

　　This story does not begin as an adaptability lesson. It begins as a story about inflexibility, both mental and physical. It's about a man whose life path has crossed mine many times. His name is Jim Turpin, and he owns the Cayman Pool Company in Phoenix, Arizona.

　　Those that know Jim usually call him "Big Jim," and for good reason. He has competed as a powerlifter for forty-four consecutive years. Weighing only

225 pounds, he squatted a whopping 722 pounds. He bench pressed 462 pounds and deadlifted 700 pounds. Fanatic that he is, he has every workout he has done since 1980 logged in his training manuals, so he can tell you what he lifted any day of any year. They don't come more dedicated than Jim Turpin, which explains how he evolved from a skinny kid with horrible rheumatoid arthritis into 225 pounds of solid muscle winning National Powerlifting Championships and breaking national records.

We first met in the Shotokan karate dojo. He recognized me from powerlifting events and introduced himself. Five or so years later, Jim prepared to test for the rank of Shodan, the first-degree black belt level. He took the test and did not pass. He trained another nine months, re-took the exam, and again did not pass. He tested a third time with the same results. Now in his late-fifties, he felt both frustration and the worry that if he couldn't pass in his late-fifties, how would he pass in his sixties? After all, this was a strict Shotokan test, evaluated by Sensei Chuck Coburn and his Sensei, Shojiro Koyama.

Finally, one night after class, I approached Jim and broached the subject. Jim Turpin has the enthusiasm of an eighteen-year-old on prom night and the pleasant demeanor of a Labrador retriever; everyone likes Jim, and everyone wanted him to pass the test. I felt the same.

"Jim," I said. "I understand powerlifting. You know that. I love powerlifting. You're a great powerlifter and I would never want to change that, but with my knowledge of powerlifting, karate, and what I do for a living, I could help you to make some modifications in your training program that will help you to pass this test. You're in your late-fifties now and it's not going to get easier. You really ought to start thinking about making some changes so you can pass this test."

"What would I have to change?" he asked.

"Well, we have to incorporate some mobility sequences for flexibility. Then we'll do some pre-hab injury prevention exercises. We'll need to lighten the weights, work on some of your stabilizing muscles and try to create some range of motion in some of the joints that have tightened over the years," I said.

I was pretty pleased with my dissertation, because I knew my assessment to be accurate. I felt sure Jim would want my help; I had twice served as the head coach of the United States powerlifting team and have been an obsessive martial artist, a black belt in the style Jim would be testing in. I thought he would tell me he'd do whatever I need him to.

"For God's sake, T-Mac; I don't want to stretch. I've been doing this for forty years now and I've won championships without doing all of that stretching and aerobics stuff. Next thing I know you're going to want to put me on the Swiss ball and I'm not going on it. We sit around and laugh at the guys using the Swiss balls while we're squatting six hundred for reps," he said.

He dumbfounded me. He had gone over forty years without stretching or aerobic training and it showed. He had the solidity of a rock—and the flexibility of a rock, too. His joint tightness caused the distinct movement sequencing problems in his karate. He had failed the test three times and was deathly afraid of being "that guy" in the gym using the Swiss ball. As said, he normally has the disposition of a loving Labrador, but now he struck me more like a raging bull—something that both shocked and amused me.

It took months, but I eroded Jim Turpin's willpower, just as the Colorado River eroded the Grand Canyon. I made minimal program changes at first, adding five minute bouts of cardiovascular training. I sold him on some mobility exercises (moving stretches), which I assured him that, all of our NFL players, Ultimate Fighters and world-class boxers used. Somehow, I even snuck the Swiss ball by him. He began to correct his forty years of bulking and tightening.

I give Jim Turpin credit. I think he would have preferred to eat his own liver than do some of what I asked him, including getting on that Swiss ball. Regardless, he did them. Despite not liking them, he did them with religious tenacity. As I hoped for, "Big Jim" saw drastic change. He maintained the muscle mass he had developed over the past forty-four years, but lost about ten pounds of body fat, making him both huge and shredded. His joints and movements became looser and more fluid. Despite the weight loss, his punches still felt like being hit by a man with a brick.

He can now wear his black belt with pride, because he earned it. He stepped up and did all of the things he didn't want to do. To this day, it pleases me to see him leave the locker room dressed in his enthusiastic demeanor and the color belt he deserves to be in. He could have only accomplished that if he adapted and did all of the things he did not want to do.

With that mission accomplished, Big Jim returned to his first love, the heavy iron. Within two years of earning his black belt, he reclaimed the National Champion title for his age group in powerlifting. He again set several national records. For my part, I am appreciative of the lesson of adaptability he afforded me, even if it meant using the dreaded Swiss ball.

Chapter 8

CLARITY OF VISION
MY UNKNOWN WOMAN

"Clarity of mind means clarity of passion, too; this is why a great and clear mind loves ardently and sees distinctly what it loves."
   -Blaise Pascal

How many times in a man's life does he see a woman and think, "I wish I knew her." I'm going to tell a story about the one that got away--the one I wish I knew.

In 2005, at the age of 45, I bowed onto the mat to fight this young hulk for the championship of the nation in ju-jitsu. I was pumped up. I was way too old, too slow and too beat up to be there, but I was three periods away from possibly being the National Champion.

Minutes later, I was on the floor, lying cold as a mackerel, the victim of knockout. The young stud kicked me so hard in the carotid artery of my neck I melted.

Once I came back from my nap on the mat, I fought on, still in hopes of pulling an upset. Whack! A thumb in the eye. Down goes Tim. Again. Only this time I wasn't asleep. I was blind. I had a very shattered cornea—one like "a windshield that is hit with a baseball," according to the doctor whom I could not see. I was withdrawn medically from that match and instead of fighting for a National Championship I was very slowly regaining a very blurry vision and placed into the loser's bracket.

I regained vision in my right eye but could barely see anything from my left when I was called to fight again. I bowed into that match with an ice bag on my eye, trying to get every last second of benefit out of that ice. I had to fight that fight left-handed because I could not really see out of my left eye and needed my good eye to be in front. I eventually ended up in third place that day. I was quite pleased with myself and sat back for a minute to admire my accomplishment.

Then I saw this girl fight. It brought me off my self-adoration trip, and back to humility.

I don't know who she is. I have tried so many times to find out who she is, but I have failed. All I know is she was a super tough fighter who fought the whole tournament, legally blind!

I wish I knew her. I would love to thank this courageous blind woman for helping me to see things so much clearer.

Chapter 9

PROBLEMS CAN BE BLESSINGS

MISTY HYMAN

"A few years' experience will convince us that those things which at the time they happened we regarded as our greatest misfortunes have proved our greatest blessings."

  -George Mason

Olympic Champion Misty Hyman (right) enjoying some time off with my wife Janet and myself.

Misty Hyman is my friend. I never had the pleasure of serving her as her coach, but I did learn a valuable lesson from her.

Misty won the 2004 Olympic Games Gold Medal for the 200-meter butterfly stroke. She upset the heavily favored Susie O'Neill of Australia. Susie was so good she had not lost a race in seven years. Imagine the great Michael Jordan leading a team that wouldn't lose for seven years. He couldn't go one year, let alone seven years, without defeat. Neither could Tiger Woods,

Wayne Gretzky, Babe Ruth or Mohammed Ali. Susie was that good, so good they nicknamed the event, "The Suzie Stroke." To achieve the seemingly impossible, Misty had to swim four seconds faster than her lifetime best. She did that.

Those that have been fortunate enough to meet Misty know she is an extreme achiever in everything she does. She has a Bachelor's degree from Stanford, of course. She owns her own business, is bilingual, kind beyond words, cute and humble. She can do it all.

That isn't the part of the story that is interesting. The interesting part was revealed when I asked her how she got started swimming. She told me when she was five years old her lung function was so poor due to asthma her doctor was quite worried she wouldn't live a normal life. He asked her mother to take her swimming as her only hope of strengthening her lungs.

In the long run, the doctor was right. If they'd never put that little, frail girl in a swimming pool, she would not have become the Misty Human we know today. She didn't end up with a normal life. She far exceeds normal in every phase of life. Isn't it great they actively intervened to help her troubles, instead of pitying and coddling her?

Misty wasn't taken to the corner to pity herself and cry about life being unfair. She was taken to a pool. Only through great effort could she show us that problems can actually be blessings in disguise: precursors to greater accomplishment.

Chapter 10

OUTSIDE THE BOX

MIKE BOTTOM

"Imagination is more important than knowledge."
  -Albert Einstein

In early 2000, I ran my business from the Phoenix Swim Club. Located near the airport, between the Biltmore and the Fashion Square districts of Phoenix, it was a perfect place to train athletes. There were ten acres, a huge football field, a full grass track, a basketball court, two Olympic pools, a sand volleyball court, and a weight room. The place belonged to former

Coach Bottom (right) giving detailed instruction to ten time Olympic medalist, Gary Hall.

world record holder and Olympic flag bearer Dr. Gary Hall, Sr. One afternoon, after his usual swim, Dr. Hall asked me if we could chat. He told me he planned to bring in an innovative swim coach and some swimmers to create a group that would train for the 2000 Olympics. He liked what I had been doing for his son, Gary Jr., and asked if I wanted to be part of the program. Gary Sr. is bright, energetic, and courteous, and so I jumped at the chance. The issue that concerned me was this innovative swim coach he mentioned. In my eyes, most swim coaches are not innovative at all. Rather they usually take the two hundred kids in their program and have them swim mega-distances until a hundred and ninety seven of tem are so burned out they no longer enjoy the sport. When three excel, they pump their chests about how good they are as coaches: it's dumbfounding.

So the day came that I met the innovative swim coach, Mike Bottom. He didn't strike me as the typical, old, stodgy American swim coach. Actually, Mike looked young and fit enough to be able to make the Olympic swim team himself. He seemed to have the word "maverick" written on him; he was an innovator.

Indeed, I found him to be a coach who thought outside the box. A specialist in training sprinters, Mike had more of an elite track coach's mentality than a swim coach's mentality. Whereas many swim coaches have fifty-meter sprinters perform four to six reps of 800-meter swims during practice, Mike had a different approach. An 800 meter swim can take fifteen minutes or more to complete, and Mike felt that sprinters, whose event lasts about twenty seconds, should concentrate at being great off the starting blocks and swimming exceptionally fast for twenty seconds. Having swimmers with predominantly fast twitch fibers (best suited for short, fast events) train in long, slow distance protocols will only hurt their ability to swim their best-suited events, while enhancing their ability to swim long, slow distances. This seems like common sense, but is not common in the world of swimming.

For Mike to apply the training methodologies as he did was unusual, and was not well received by many of the swim coaches in the country. Undaunted, Bottom spent countless hours thinking and formulating his programs and had tremendous courage to go against what everyone else regarded as right. Mike thought way outside the box. Together we constructed an innovative strength training program using boxing techniques, martial arts techniques, speed drills, speed ladder drills and football-like plyometric drills.

I loved working with Mike. He had the genius to think outside the box and the strength to remain true to his programs despite their unusual and often "unacceptable" nature. And he achieved phenomenal results with those programs, not only with Gary Hall Jr. (the world's fastest swimmer for two Olympic Games) but also with Anthony Ervin (another gold medalist) and the rest of the group. His example of thinking for himself in the best interest of others, instead of conforming blindly will always live on in a place in my heart.

Chapter 11

▲

HELPING OUT A BROTHER

BRIAN DAWKINS

"We must learn to live together as brothers or perish together as fools."
  -Martin Luther King

One particularly hot summer afternoon in Phoenix, we had about twenty NFL players in our run group. Donovan McNabb, Keith Bulluck, Aeneas Williams, Brian Westbrook, Brian Dawkins, Antwaan Randle-El and several others made the session quite dynamic. Something about their energy that day persuaded me to make the session longer and more intense than usual.

After the session, many players jumped in the pool and then sat beneath the shade of the trees drinking Gatorade and discussing the intensity of the workout. Everyone felt the exhaustion, but such was the sense of accomplishment that everyone was happy, too. Players like Donovan get a high from that sort of workout. They feel if they can put out that kind of work in 110-degree heat, they'll certainly be able to handle practice conditions just about anywhere.

One of the guys, Brian Dawkins, worked incredibly hard that day. Brian had come out with about nine other members of the Philadelphia Eagles at Donovan's invitation. Brian Dawkins is the sort of player every strength and conditioning coach wants to work with. He came for one reason, to become his best. While others throughout the league slept or took vacation time that day, the world's top free safety was working like an unknown kid just trying to make a roster. He completed every drill with purpose and demanded perfection of himself. He had clearly ascended to the top of the league by sheer effort.

He and Donovan and I sat under the tree talking about the traits the separate great players from good players, traits like focus, desire, pain tolerance and self-belief. After a half an hour or so, we noticed everyone else had left. There was only the three of us and the thirty or more Gatorade bottles littered everywhere. Donovan asked if I was going to take off, and I told him I would head back to the weight room once I cleaned up the bottles.

"Hang on Tim, I'll get it," he said, taking me by surprise. The best quarterback in the game had just volunteered to clean up trash left by not only his teammates, but also the college players and high school kids who ran with us that day.

"Hey Reggie," Donovan called out across the fifty meter pool to Reggie Brown. Reggie had just been signed out of the University of Georgia as a high draft pick of the Eagles. As Reggie walked the length of the pool towards us I wondered why Donovan continued to sit there and why he yelled for Reggie.

Without saying a word Reggie did what he was supposed to do. He started to pick up the Gatorade bottles. This is a rite of passage for many sports organizations, where the rookies are assigned unwritten tasks of carrying playbooks, buying dinners or doing menial things such as cleaning up Gatorade bottles. Without hesitation and without signs of malcontent, this great guy, rookie Reggie Brown, went to work.

I admit to laughing excessively at Donovan's ingenuity. This was classic Donovan McNabb, a fun loving guy who could reach right into your heart.

As I sat admiring Donovan's genius, I watched Reggie pick up bottle after bottle. Brian Dawkins, the top free safety in the game, jumped up and said, "I'll help my brother." And he did. He jumped up in a manner uncharacteristic of veterans, let alone All-Pro players, and picked up the trash. In my eyes, Brian Dawkins instantly became more than just an All-Pro player. He became an All-Pro person.

I admit to feeling embarrassed at that moment, when I realized this great player had jumped in to help someone he considered a brother when I did not.

I was too busy admiring Donovan's cunning to help out a man who could use help.

I learned a lesson that day. Well, actually I learned a couple of lessons. I learned that Donovan is a little more cunning than I thought, but more importantly, I learned by example a lesson about helping out a brother. Thank you, Brian Dawkins, for showing me greatness both on and off the field.

Chapter 12

REPETITION

SENSEI DAN

"Repetition may be boring, but at the same time it can be very enlightening. How often, for instance, do we use the alphabet, or multiplication tables?"
   -Gary B. Wright

Sensei Dan throwing one of his many opponents during his 30 years in judo.

Dan Sisson and I happened to attend the same judo school one night over twenty years ago—at school that neither of us attended regularly. We did an hour and half of drills together, and somehow that sufficed to form a life friendship.

Dan had already earned his black belt and I wasn't there yet. That night, he provided extra guidance to me. As our friendship grew, we began training together on weekends outside of class, and Dan always gave me considerable feedback and critique, for which I will always be grateful. His kindness and love for the art of judo drove him to teach me and help me perform throws, many times with him being the guy taking the falls.

"Do it again," he said often, when I made mistakes. Judo, the art of throwing, pinning, choking, and arm locking an opponent into submission, is far more difficult to learn than the striking arts, which require kicks and punches. Pulling a man forward, particularly one who doesn't want to be thrown, while turning your back to him, has inherent difficulty.

"Do it again," I heard over and over, every time I had a foot, a hand, an arm, or my hips as little as an inch out of position. With time, and because of Sensei Dan's careful teaching, I started to get better. I was learning over sixty throws, and several variations of each, and I found myself getting them wrong a bit less often.

"Do it again, that was really good," he started to say. Enthused by this tough critic's show of approval, I felt better and realized my judo had finally reached a standard I had previously hoped for. Then it dawned on me, that in spite of the improvement, Sensei Dan still asked me to "do it again."

"Sensei Dan, when it wasn't very good, I had to do it again. Now that you say it is pretty good, and you're still telling me to do it again. I don't get it."

"When it was bad, you needed the repetitions to make it good. Now that it is getting good, you need the repetitions to ensure that it becomes a proper habit. You always need the repetitions. Repetitions enable you to go from bad to good and will someday take you from good to great," he said.

I learned this from my friend, my Sensei "do it again" Dan. I often use these words of wisdom on the athletes I instruct. Without fail, the "do it again" theory seems to validate itself. Thank you, Sensei Dan, and please know the lesson of repetition, as per your instruction, has been passed on over and over and over again.

Mike Koerner taking one of the falls that you just don't want to do again.

Chapter 13

AN EXTRA FIVE MINUTES

MIKE VANARSDALE

"The difference between the ordinary and the extraordinary is the extra."
    -Anonymous

Mike (right) instructing a future champion.
He knows the road to get there.

During his prime, Mike VanArsdale was a National Junior Wrestling Champion, a National Collegiate Athletic Association National Champion and the Freestyle World Cup Champion. He later pursued a career in mixed martial arts, in the mid 1990s, when popular belief held that Brazilians could not be beaten in mixed martial arts. Without a great deal of training, Mike fought in a tournament in Brazil and beat three stand-out Brazilian fighters all in the same night, by three different methods. He beat one guy by knocking him out. He dislocated the shoulder of another after a high amplitude throw. He choked the third unconscious. Mike was that good as an athlete.

Mike VanArsdale was also good at sports outside of grappling. He played high school basketball and was a standout football player. Beyond Mike's athletic side, though, is much more.

A father of five, every time I see him interact with his children I think he's some sort of super dad. He is also quite funny. A keen observer, he can quite accurately mimic the voice, movement patters, and idiosyncrasies of everyone he comes in contact with. At the Olympic wrestling training camps in 1996, I remember Mike entertaining a room of fifteen wrestlers with stories and imitations for three straight hours. We laughed until we cried, in awe of how Mike knew every little nuance of everyone in USA wrestling. The following night he somehow told the exact same group the exact same stories and we all sat and laughed as if we had heard them for the first time. Those same guys met for the third night in a row and all laughed hysterically again. I swore to myself I would not go down and hear the same stand-up routine for a third consecutive night and would go to my dorm room to write lifting programs, but everyone's laughter drew me there. I went to both the third and fourth nights. If camp hadn't ended, I might still be going.

As if being a superb athlete, father and comedian weren't enough, Mike VanArsdale is just a good person, and one I know who will be a great friend for life. Today, he is probably the top coach in mixed martial arts, leading many fighters to World Championships and unparalleled success.

I have an appreciation for people who excel in a variety of endeavors. I know how many people are enamored with that guy who can shoot a basketball or hit a baseball. I don't find that all that impressive. I think everyone should probably have one skill or interest that they've cultivated. The people who impress me are those who achieve in many areas, like Mike.

Mike (right) sharing a good time with my coach, Doug Jepperson.

The lesson I learned from Mike VanArsdale was simple. One day as we sat after judo training I asked him about the key to his success.

"Five minutes, McClellan," he said, in his usual enthusiastic voice. Oh boy, here we go with another VanArsdale-ism, I thought. What on earth is this nut up to now? I wondered.

"I show up and train hard five minutes before everybody else does. I stay after practice and train hard five minutes after everyone else does. It's a very intense five minutes, but it's only five minutes. While everyone else is not practicing, I get in a total of ten extra minutes per day. In a six-day training week, that gives me an extra hour. That means I get four to five extra hours per month and fifty to fifty-two hours a year depending on vacations. I've been doing that for over twenty years. Imagine what a jump I have had over competitors whom have not done this for twenty years."

It was a simple lesson. I had asked a simple question, and I got a simple answer. And although I've never seen it, I am sure Mike VanArsdale can imitate the astonishment on my face when he told me this lesson that I now apply to not only my training, but to the rest of my life as well. Thank you, Mike VanArsdale, for teaching me the value of an extra five minutes.

Chapter 14

DOING IT ALL AND DOING IT ALL RIGHT
NICOLE POWELL

"Perhaps the most valuable result of all education is the ability to make yourself do the thing you have to do when it ought to be done, whether you like it or not; it is the first lesson that ought to be learned."
      -Thomas H. Huxley

The ultra successful Nicole Powell with President Bush.

My friend Nicole Powell is one of those extraordinary people who does everything well. She does everything with passion and effort, and in doing so, has reached unusual levels of accomplishment. Nicole grew up in Phoenix where she attended Mountain Pointe High School. There she was the state champion in discus. She ran the eight hundred meters and was a member of the four by eight hundred meter relay team, which placed second in state championships. She was the three time state champion in badminton and a state runner up in tennis. In basketball, she was named the Arizona Player of the Century and the Arizona Female Athlete of the Year. Are these the signs of a great athlete? Obviously. Did genetics play a role in these accomplishments? Definitely. But she wasn't just a great athlete. She maintained high grades and was admitted to Stanford University on scholarship. And then, as if great grades and excellence in badminton, basketball, tennis, discus, cross country, and track weren't enough, she earned a varsity letter as a member of the band. This should give you an idea of how special Nicole Powell really is.

Nicole Powell had great genetics, but I've seen plenty of athletes with similar gifts. Nicole Powell is special because she simply tries hard and does everything with extraordinary diligence. This is why she had a chance to play in the Woman's Junior World Championships, why she broke several school records at Stanford, why she graduated from such a prestigious university, and why she was a first round pick in the WNBA. Nicole has been part of a WNBA championship team, and as such, has been honored at the White House. She has competed and toured all over the world in the WNBA off-season.

Noted inspirational speaker Anthony Robbins said in his book, *Unlimited Power*, that to be successful, people should "stretch" themselves. Nicole Powell is not afraid to accept new challenges and stretch herself. She stretched herself and her Stanford teammates by bringing them to Phoenix and running in 100-degree heat, sessions in which she herself would end up puking. These were also sessions that were immediately followed by demanding weight room workouts. These were also sessions she could have skipped – she was away from the confines of the mandatory program at Stanford and could have simply told the coaches at Stanford she was doing her workouts in Phoenix. Rather, she accepted many challenges, and found ways to excel at them all.

I look back with great sadness at the times when athletes end their careers having left behind so much room for development -- and wish they could have had the blessing of observing Nicole as I have. That's why I wasted no time introducing Nicole to a twelve-year old aspiring basketball player, Courtney Ekmark, whom I suspected wanted to have a successful career like Nicole. My

hope was that Nicole would share wisdom on how to achieve results above and beyond others.

As per my hope, Nicole gladly met with Courtney and did an outstanding job of counseling her. It was well above and beyond what I would have suspected. It could be no other way for Nicole Powell.

Chapter 15

EXECUTION

KEVIN RAYES

"Quality is never an accident; it is always the result of high intention, sincere effort, intelligent direction and skillful execution; it represents the wise choice of many alternatives."

    -William A. Foster

It is fitting that Kevin Rayes runs track...a sport where Nike's shoes popularized the slogan, "Just do it." Kevin "just does it."

I first met Kevin his junior year in high school. He wanted me to help him prepare for his senior year. It wasn't long before I recognized that this kid did everything I asked him to the very best of his ability, 100% of

Kevin Rayes winning a race not off natural ability but off execution.

the time. This included the very difficult training sessions I prescribed (multiple timed intervals in varying distances where he surprisingly hit the precise time plus or minus one second every time), precise diets (counting grams of protein, eating at timed intervals) and even race times (hitting to the second the exact times I prescribed as we gradually lowered them in the four events he ran throughout the season).

It has been said "execution beats emotion." Kevin Rayes simply executed every phase of his training, every day. He sat in the cold tub every time I prescribed it. He ate a perfect diet, was perfect in his supplementation program, worked on the foam roller exactly as prescribed and logged each of his training runs in great detail. Even his one-mile race in the state finals was executed to perfection. I asked him to run the first lap in exactly 67 seconds, regardless of his place among the field. He did so and was 15th of 16 runners. He was asked to come through the halfway mark at 2:12, which he did exactly. He was 13th of out 16. Anyone else would have freaked out being that far back, but Kevin never got emotional. He simply executed. He finished that race (not his best event) in a personal record and in second place. Best of all, the following week he won the Arizona Meet of Champions (all runners of all levels) in his event, the 800 meters in a personal best time of 1:52, six full seconds faster than the previous year.

Truthfully, it was a bizarre experience for me to coach Kevin. I coached him for two full years on a daily basis and not once did he ever deviate from his course of execution. Granted, I have had dozens of very coachable, trusting athletes that worked along the same line, but never have I seen someone follow thousands of very detailed directions and execute them all to perfection, with little or no emotion. Essentially he never got in his own way, as we all do too often.

In the end, this once average runner with an unmatched ability to execute

earned a partial scholarship to run at the University of Texas. His success would have been unfathomable to me when I first coached him, but then again, his ability to execute would have been unfathomable as well. I'll never see another like him, although I'd sure love to.

Chapter 16

▲

GRINDING EVERY DAY
CHARLIE FRYE

"The process to attain mastery is long and tedious. There is no way to perfection but through patience and super-human effort."
-From the martial arts documentary, "Budo"

Most people don't consider University of Akron a quarterback factory the way they might think of the University of Southern California. The University of Akron has not been considered the pinnacle of football success. Still, Charlie Frye went through the University of Akron as a quarterback and became the starting NFL quarterback for the Cleveland Browns, the Seattle Seahawks, and the Oakland Raiders.

I was blessed to see this transformation, from college kid to starting NFL quarterback, and I know just how Charlie achieved his success. He wanted it more than others.

I met Charlie in January after his senior season because his agent wanted us to prepare him for the NFL Scouting Combine. A blue-collar kid, I suspected him of being the type to do some serious work in the weight room. In our first conversation, I sat in the corner of the gym with Charlie, his agent, and his father, for more than an hour. Charlie said nothing until the meeting ended—literally nothing for over an hour when we were talking about his future. Finally, he said, "I'll do whatever you want. I promise you that." That was all he said.

Indeed, he did whatever was asked of him—and more. In fact, he probably doubled the work we asked of him, which was a lot to begin with. He showed up daily at 8:00 a.m. and stretched until 8:30. On the field, we would go through the intense daily running workouts, which lasted an hour and a half. After, he would stay another two hours and throw footballs to receivers in our combine training group. After throwing, he dipped in the pool to bring his core body temperature down. Then, he ate a lunch of precisely prescribed foods before he met with offensive genius and former NFL head coach Rod Dowhower. Rod and Charlie would watch game films for two or three hours, sometimes more. Then he reported for his weight room workouts. Charlie did not lift like a pampered quarterback; he gave everything he had for up to two hours. Then he made a beeline back to Rod Dowhower, with whom, on most days, he would go out on the field and throw for a second session of two more hours. When he did not throw for a second session, he would watch more films. In a few weeks, all of the wide receivers started wearing out. Charlie wanted to throw as much as possible and needed people to run routes for him to throw to; he put them all in a state of overtraining. Weeks later, we started to wear out too. I pride myself as a coach with more energy than the athletes, and in that way, a positive influence, but maintaining Charlie's pace became a battle. He put the Energizer Bunny to shame. The wide receivers called it quits, saying they would run routes with him once a day and no more. Charlie still wanted to throw twice a day, and enlisted the help of defensive backs and running backs, who could run. He somehow talked them into running pass patterns for him as wide receivers--until he wore them out.

At the end of the combine training season, which went about eight weeks, Charlie Frye became an offensive genius under Rod Dowhower's guidance.

His passing accuracy improved and he could throw a ball seven yards further than he had ever thrown in his life, an astounding ten percent performance enhancement increase. The Cleveland Browns drafted him in the third round, and everyone expected him to intern his way into a backup role. Indeed, he started as a backup, but was soon named the Brown's starting quarterback. He later went on to start games for the Seattle Seahawks and Oakland Raiders.

What a pleasure to work with the NFL's two hardest working quarterbacks: Charlie Frye (left) and Donovan McNabb (right).

Many wonder where this kid from Akron came from. He epitomized the athletic rags-to-riches story. Nevertheless, those of us in Phoenix knew he had performed no overnight miracle. We are all still recovering from Hurricane Charlie, amazed to see a person who will not bend before any obstacle, regardless of exhaustion or difficulty. I am blessed to have seen Charlie Frye's miraculous efforts. I wish everyone had the privilege of watching him grind every day, without fail.

Chapter 17

THE DAY THE EXCUSES ENDED

ANTHONY ROBLES

"The future belongs to those who believe in the beauty of their dreams."
-Eleanor Roosevelt

For several years, I had heard stories about a local wrestler, Anthony Robles. Anthony grew up in Mesa, Arizona, a neighboring town to where I live. He later attended Arizona State University, which is close proximity to my home. Even though I had heard these miraculous, inspiring stories of his ability on that mat, I had never ventured out to see him wrestle. Once I did, I could not stop. I got addicted. It was a mindboggling, jaw-dropping experience that defies my ability to convey its specialty through written words.

Anthony's story, as I write it, ends in Philadelphia in March 2011. I was there, at the National Collegiate Athletic Association's National Championships. This was the last meet of Anthony's senior season and represented the 37th match he would wrestle that year. It would also be the 37th match he would win, culminating his perfect, undefeated season in which he became the PAC-10

Champion, National Champion and the Outstanding Wrestler at the National Championships. In short, he could not have done better.

To look at Anthony, you would seemingly see a young, strong, focused athlete who just conveys a sense of happiness and peace. The many friends I have that know him could not speak more highly of his training ethic, focus or caring, friendly demeanor off the mat. Indeed, what you see is what you get. He's just a great human being.

But, as Paul Harvey used to say, "now the rest of the story." Anthony Robles made all these miraculous accomplishments despite having only one leg to wrestle on. He was born that way. Yes, of the 330 wrestlers that competed in Philadelphia, 329 had two legs, yet the only one with one leg was the one we'll always remember. It was indescribable.

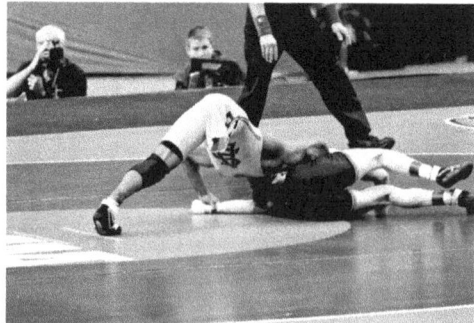

For me, Anthony Robles put an end to all of my excuses, such as my herniated discs acting up, my broken bones, and my tired 52-year old body that is severely over-trained.

I cannot imagine what his mother Judith felt when her little boy with one leg said he wanted to go to wrestling practice. Imagine that. Wrestlers hurt their legs so frequently, many times severely enough to require surgery. If Anthony were to do that, he wouldn't have a leg left to stand on. It must have been so hard for both of them, but thank you Judith, thank you Anthony. There never were excuses with either of you-only results. You both have gone where others have not and your example will lead others to glorious new heights.

The top 8 finalists at the 2011 NCAA Championships.

Chapter 18

SEEKING OPTIMIZATION

HIROSHI ALLEN

"The man on top of the mountain didn't get there by chance."
  -Unknown

Hiroshi Allen is a master of Karate. At age 39 he has trained his art intensely for 34 years. His travels for training and competition have led him around the world: to Japan, the Czech Republic, the Dominican Republic, Brazil, Canada, Germany, France and the Philippines. The son of two amazing black belt practitioners, Bob Allen and Nikki Ikeda, he has seen it all.

During his travels Hiroshi has collected a few notable titles such as 3-time World Champion and 17-time National Champion. He now owns a dojo in Las Vegas, where he trains his students to achieve the successes he has had. There isn't much he didn't accomplish while competing on the mat.

Off the mat, his education helps his students as well. Having been trained in the exercise physiology major for his Master's Degree studies, Hiroshi spent years under the tutelage of David Richardson, then strength and conditioning coach of the University of Louisiana at Monroe, now of the Ohio State University. He has spent the better portion of his last 20 years studying off-mat training concepts. He has superior knowledge and ability both on-and-off the competition mat.

In 2012, Hiroshi decided to stage a comeback to competition, after retiring several years earlier. He asked me to help him.

To me, that said it all. Instead of simply constructing training protocols himself, which he is certainly qualified to do; he sought outside help in attempt to optimize his performance.

As a result of Hiroshi's example, I have made a vow to always seek more guidance, more wisdom and knowledge. If a guy who won 3 World Championships and 17 National Championships did it, I should too.

▲

Chapter 19

LEAVING NO STONE UNTURNED

DARRIN SCHENCK

"A person should not be measured by what they accomplish, but what they overcome."

    -Johnny Miller

    Darrin Schenck wrote the book on racquetball training, literally. His book, *Percentage Racquetball*, is often regarded as the top text in the field. Schenck's concept for succeeding at racquetball is built on a system of percentages. The application of this concept enabled him to have a successful career on the International Racquetball tour. He spent three years in the top twenty-five worldwide, with a career high, season-end ranking of eighteen.

    The accomplishments are especially impressive given that he started so late, by his own account in *Percentage Racquetball*. He didn't see a racquetball court until he reached fifteen, whereas most touring professionals start at age eight. He had a small fraction of their training time. Furthermore, he did not come from an affluent family, so private lessons with respected pros were out of the question. He also weighed in at a slight 134 pounds. So how did Darrin achieve extraordinary success when so many factors were stacked

against him?

First, he spent an inordinate amount of time on the racquetball court and he enlisted the services of a competent strength and conditioning coach. He studied martial arts under Ja Shin Do Master Andy Bauman to improve fitness, flexibility, self-control and self-discipline. He worked with a hypnotherapist to improve his mental approach to competition. He traded out racquetball lessons with a massage therapist to help him recover from training. Furthermore, he graduated from a sports vision therapy program in Scottsdale, Arizona and went east to train under Andy Roberts, the former number one World Tour pro. Darrin left no stone unturned.

I coached Darrin through these years and am inspired by his efforts. If an average guy with all the odds stacked against him can rise to world prominence, others can as well. They just need to follow his lead and leave no stone unturned.

▲

Chapter 20

HUMILITY

DEION SANDERS

"The squeaky wheel gets the grease."
　-Unknown

　　A pro-football cornerback has one of the toughest jobs in sports. Mirroring every running pattern of wide-receivers—who themselves can run forty yards in under four and a half seconds--is hard enough. But to do so backwards, while keeping an eye on that receiver and the quarterback, makes it the king of all athletic challenges. Deion Sanders was a pro-football cornerback. He did all of that and did it well. In fact, he did it better than anybody of his era, and perhaps as well as anybody in history. And he had incomparable punt returning and kick-returning skills to boot. He could catch a ball that had been punted sixty yards into the air while defenders barreled down at him at blazing speeds, avoid eleven tacklers, and then run over seventy yards to a touchdown.

　　As if that weren't enough, he was almost as good at baseball. Few athletes have the chance to play in the World Series. Few athletes have the fortune to play in the Super Bowl. Deion Sanders did both.

　　Many stories have been told about Deion Sanders. A good friend of mine, Rich Aurilia, still talks about how Deion encouraged him sixteen years ago, when Rich was unknown, recently called up to play major league baseball, and Deion was a veteran player. Rich was the scared rookie in the big league clubhouse and Deion's support meant a lot to him.

　　Then there are the stories that portray Deion as conceited. I don't know Deion well, so I can't comment on the accuracy of those. But too many times in my career I've seen media and critics take unwarranted pot shots at a star athlete's character. (For example, I wrote a chapter in *Inner Strength Inner Peace* about how I found Olympic gold medalist Gary Hall Jr. to be warm, humble, hardworking and thankful—and yet the media sometimes portrayed him as a loose cannon who didn't train hard.)

The only claims I will make about Deion come from personal experience. Years ago, during his first (brief) retirement, Deion worked as a television commentator for NFL games. He was sent to do a piece on how we trained football player Donovan McNabb and dozens other professional players. Deion arrived early and presented himself as a professional and a Southern gentleman. We spoke for half an hour before the athletes arrived, ready to start their running session in the famous hundred-and-five degree Phoenix heat. Deion asked to go through the workout, to get a feel for what the players went through. I told him we would be honored to have him, and that we had some rules that governed all drills. For example, each drill began behind the designated start line and finished past the designated finishing line. Each athlete should step up to take his turn without delay and do each drill without hitting the equipment used, such as the agility ladders, bags, cones or mini-hurdles. Partway through the workout, I was admiring Deion's gift of athleticism when he actually hit one of our hurdles.

"New guy, get down and do your push-ups," I called out to him. We assign all our athletes push-ups to deter inappropriate execution.

"How many, sir?" he asked.

He surprised me with his humility, especially in front of a group of lesser athletes. He had responded like a new recruit into the freshman class of the United States Military Academy. This man who had conquered the toughest job in pro sports, had made teams punt away from him as a punt returner and had also played in the World Series—though he didn't have the opportunity to play as much baseball as everyone else in the league—was willing to let some guy he had met only forty minutes earlier put him down to do push-ups by himself in front of many of the top athletes in the world, and many young kids he did not know. Afterwards I thanked him for joining our workout and for rolling with the punches of my style in making him do push-ups. He thanked me and told me he thought it important that he be treated like everyone else in the group, so not to compromise the quality of our workout.

I later had the chance to watch his interview of Donovan McNabb. Deion floored me. Thoroughly professional, he had clearly spent an inordinate amount of time preparing for the interview, as he knew all of the stats and everything else one could possibly know of Donovan's career.

I enjoyed working with Deion Sanders. As a strength and conditioning coach, I love seeing athletes whose performance is off the charts. I appreciated his professional approach, and the extensive amount of preparation he did before coming to Phoenix. And besides, I got a kick out of telling my friends I made Deion Sanders do push-ups for hitting my hurdle. Best of all, though, in that two-hour period of my life, I learned the valuable lesson of humility from perhaps the greatest athlete of our generation.

Chapter 21

GETTING RESOLUTION

RAY BOURQUE

"All the so-called "secrets of success" will not work unless you do."
    -Unknown

The first day I worked with the Boston Bruins during their off-season strength and conditioning program, they were testing their abilities in various lifts and runs. The first guy I talked to was a future NHL Hall of Famer, Ray Bourque. I was stunned. This was late into his career and we all knew he would soon be a Hall of Famer. Yet he was asking me, an unknown, what he should do for his warm-ups before his bench press max test. It was so respectful and trusting I still smile when I picture it. He just wanted that badly to do things properly. It was all about successful resolution for Ray Bourque—nothing else.

Watching him practice for the next month was magical, nothing less. Ray wasn't born with superhuman genetics. He achieved superhuman results. He made mistakes. He got beat. Every athlete does. The difference between Ray Bourque and others was that he would only make a mistake once. I sat every day for one month straight watching him deliberately move himself up in lines to challenge the best offensive players the Bruins had. He did this on every drill, every day. When one would get the best of him, he would see where they were in their line and finagle his way in his line to do a re-match. He won every re-match, every day, all month. He just had to get it right. There was no other way for him. He just had to win.

It was no surprise he won the puck shooting contest at the NHL All-Star Game Skills Competition. It's a matter of doing things properly and no one in the game could do that better than Ray Bourque. He just did more of it and would stop at nothing short of resolution.

I wish every athlete I had ever coached could have lived the lesson from this man of focus. I'd have more stories to write on champions if they had.

Chapter 22

KEEPING THE INNER FIRE

TRIP HEDRICK

"The miracle, or the power, that elevates the few is to be found in their industry, application and perseverance under the prompting of a brave, determined spirit."

-Mark Twain

I toured the Iowa State University athletic facility about fifteen years ago. Trip Hedrick was the head swim coach for the men's team at that time and I remember coming away from our conversation astounded by how cutting-edge his swimming and strength training programs were. He wasn't just thinking outside the box. He had ditched the box. Best of all, he had achieved out-of-the-box results as well. When I asked him about this, he said, "Think about it, Tim. I don't get the best recruits to come to Ames, Iowa. I start with lesser-talented individuals and so I have to think outside the box and provide better guidance so that the teams will be competitive with the more appealing programs." That's exactly what he did.

Years later, Iowa State sadly dropped their men's swimming program and Trip went to work for Championship Productions. He asked me if I had interest in providing strength and conditioning instructional videos and I jumped at the opportunity. I knew I would learn by collaborating with an innovator like Trip and the experience was quite the blessing. We shot about a dozen videos, their subject matter ranging from technical instruction on the power clean to speed and agility training for all athletes. They have done well in sales and I enjoyed the production process.

I love picking Trip's brain and exchanging ideas on training philosophy and athlete mentorship. It is great feedback from not only an outstanding coach -- but also someone who has watched videos and film shoots of all the elite coaches.

To this day, he continues to compete as a Masters' Level swimmer. He has won individual national championships and world championships. He has shattered world records and has been part of relay teams that have won world championships and broken world records. Like his coaching, his competitive results are atypical. They have been for decades and still are today. I am struck most by Trip's enthusiasm for swimming though. When I talk to him on the phone, I can feel his passion, though he is some two thousand miles away. I feel motivated and enlightened. His passion for swimming makes a difference in my karate and judo. Before long, I feel the compelling urge to call him, not to talk about future video projects, but for exposure to that fire he still has burning for his swimming. From Trip I have learned to rekindle my inner fire, something I try to share with all of my athletes.

Chapter 23

DEDICATION

TRISHA SAUNDERS

"Self-sacrifice is the real miracle out of which all the reported miracles grow."

-Ralph Waldo Emerson

In earliest memories of Trisha Saunders, in the late 1980s, she was running around the wrestling mats at Arizona State University, still unmarried and going by her maiden name Trisha McNaughton. Her appearance drew attention. Slim, muscular, with beautiful long blond hair, we saw her often at wrestling matches and speculated she was a wrestler's girlfriend. We did not guess she was a wrestler herself, or that she would win more World Championships than anyone associated with ASU's wrestling program at the time. That includes legendary coach Bobby Douglas, Olympic gold medalist Kenny Monday, assistant coach and Olympic Silver Medalist Zeke Jones, future Olympic silver medalist Townsend Saunders, and several others nationally renowned freestyle wrestling superstars.

Not long after my initial sightings of Trisha, I found her to be a dedicated, hardworking, and self-sacrificing athlete. I would finish working around seven-thirty every night and I would hear a radio blaring from the wrestling room next door. I always popped my head in because I worked with Bobby Douglas, then ASU's wrestling coach, and all of the members of his team. I found Trisha there every night, without fail, for years.

Later, she married Townsend Saunders, and they were blessed with a baby girl. Trish couldn't wrestle during pregnancy, but she always exercised.

Then, as per common sense and doctors' orders, she disappeared, late in the pregnancy. A week after Townsend and Trisha had their baby girl, I strolled by the wrestling room, and heard the music blaring. I wondered who would be training at eight on a Friday night, and so I went in. At first the room looked empty, but then I saw two people. Trisha was riding the exercise bike, and her new daughter, Tassia, was in a stroller on the mat.

"Trish, are you okay?"

"Yeah, Tim. I want to wrestle at the World Championships this year and I missed some training time with the pregnancy. So I know I need to catch up."

She certainly caught up. Trisha went on to win four World Wrestling Championships. I am sure none of the women she beat ever knew that only one week after giving birth, Trisha Saunders was back training, but I did. It is a lesson of how unusual dedication can cause unusual success, and one I'll never forget.

Chapter 24

PERSONAL DISCIPLINE

ZACH MILLER

"Perhaps the most valuable result of all education is the ability to make yourself do the thing you have to do, when it ought to be done, whether you like it or not; it is the first lesson that ought to be learned."

    -Unknown

I met Zach Miller when he was barely twenty-one. He was leaving college after his true junior season to enter the NFL draft. Many athletes play five full seasons in college, four as an active player and one as a "redshirt." To play only three seasons, as Zach had done, is rare.

I had heard of Zach long before I met him. He played high school football at Desert Vista High School in the Phoenix area, and my good friend Jeff Decker was their strength and conditioning coach as well as the football team's defensive coordinator. Jeff helped build a powerhouse team, a team that at one point won twenty-one consecutive games, was ranked fifth in the nation, and had seven players in one senior class sign Division I NCAA scholarships. Zach, an underclassman at that time, was a huge factor in their success. Virtually every major college in the country recruited him and he finally decided to play at Arizona State University to be close to friends and family.

Zach caught more than fifty passes his freshman year of college and played like a beast during the next two seasons. He was named to almost every post-season All-American team presented, including First Team Honors in the prestigious Walter Camp All-American team.

I finally met Zach when he evaluated our facility to see if it would fit his needs in preparation for the 2007 NFL Invitational Scouting Combine. For the NFL Combine, about two hundred draft-eligible players go to Indianapolis for four days of ultra-intense performance-related screening measures. They undergo six hours of physicals, x-rays, MRIs, psychological questionnaires, speed and agility tests, strength tests, height, weight, flexibility and body composition measures—including even measurements of their hand span. Players spend a total of four days, sleeping two to four hours per night, while being prodded, probed or psychologically challenged the other twenty hours. I have prepared athletes for the Combine for more than twenty years, so I felt confident I could benefit Zach.

The day after this meeting, Zach decided it was a fit and we started work. Much like the day before, Zach remained quiet but focused on his workout. We had only five weeks and after taking Zach's pre-test measures of bodyweight, bench pressing 225 pounds for maximum number of reps, vertical jump and standing long jump, I knew we had an immense amount of work to do. Zach was an absolute beast on the football field, but his test measures were not outstanding so I was concerned it would throw up a huge flag to NFL evaluators. If he went to the Combine and posted the measures he posted in front of me, he would risk dropping draft status, which can literally cost a player a million dollars or more in the tenure of his first contract.

Zach had signed with Athletes First, an agency out of California, to represent him. Their agents have represented some of the biggest names in pro football. I found their entire staff friendly, driven and extremely professional. Everyone I met and interviewed gave me the impression that they care for their athletes and wanted Zach to have the best of everything. They gave me the carte blanche approval to do as I needed to optimize the performance of their client. Feeling fully trusted and eager to get results, I went to work.

The first guy I contacted was Tom Incledon, the guy I call the smartest man on earth. Tom founded the company Human Performance Specialists and works as a sports nutrition scientist. Zach weighed only 243 pounds and didn't have a prototypical muscular appearance so we needed nutritional intervention. Tom detailed every bite of food that went into Zach's mouth for the next seven weeks, which took him through both the NFL Combine and his individual workout days with pro scouts. According to Tom's program, Zach would eat seven meals a day. Each gram of protein, fat, and carbohydrate was carefully calculated. Tom drew up an extensive list of supplements and a regimen detailing exactly what time of day each piece of food and supplement could be taken. Tom arranged for all meals to be created and prepared to his specifications each morning. I enjoyed watching this process of creating the ultimate diet and looked forward to seeing the outcome of his planning.

Seven weeks later, I saw that outcome. In those seven weeks he went from 243 to 256 pounds. His once large physique had become both larger and chiseled. He had gained thirteen pounds but his waist looked two to three inches smaller, his vertical jump increased more than four inches, his standing long jump by a foot, his bench press reps at 225 pounds almost doubled and he lowered his forty yard dash time by approximately three-tenths of a second.

But the story doesn't end there. This story isn't about an athlete's physical progress, because I expect my athletes to make progress. I hold myself personally accountable for their results. This story is about an athlete with incredible personal-discipline.

When all was said and done and I had established a close relationship with Zach, I asked him, "Zach, tell me honestly, did you ever get far off the diet?"

"No," he said.

"Well did you ever go to Taco Bell or have pizza or binge?"

"No, Tim. Not one bite this whole time. The only things that went in my mouth were exactly what Tom wanted."

I had posed this question seven weeks into our training. For seven consecutive weeks, Zach ate breakfast #1 at exactly 7:45, if that had been prescribed. When asked to take Tom's supplement Neuropath, designed to quicken brainwave transmission, Zach did exactly that. When asked to have a Muscle Milk protein drink with a cup of blackberries at 2:15 p.m., he followed orders to perfection.

Zach Miller came to us with a long list of accolades, but was never any sort of prima donna. He didn't have the intense motor of Simeon Rice or the change of direction of Antwaan Randle-El . What he did have is amazing personal discipline. He does what he ought to do, when he ought to do it, how he ought to do it, without deviation. It is no doubt why he became an All-American as a collegian and All-Pro as a professional. As for me, given the choice I'd much rather have those accolades than all of the junk food in the world. So would Zach Miller.

Chapter 25

▲

LETTING GO

KYLIE HUTSON

"Learn to let go. That is the key to happiness."
   -The Buddha

I've never met anyone like Kylie Hutson before. Seriously, she's unique. It's not the fact that she's funny, fit, cute and personable—I've met lots of those folks. It is the fact that the minute she is done with her athletic practice, she literally leaves it all behind. It's all gone.

I, on the other hand, as my teammates can attest, can stay mad at my performance for hours, days, weeks, even months. At times, when it gets really bad, I refuse to don my black belt and demote myself to white belt, the ones beginners wear.

Kylie, however, lets it all go. It has been said in sports sometimes success depends not on what the athlete remembers (huge successes) but rather on what they can forget (referring to the mistakes and losses).

This is not a remarkable story, one where the gal expected to be last actually wins...well, unless you consider this: Kylie Hutson had a collegiate personal best vault of 4.50 meters (approximately 14 feet, 9 inches). Her first year out of college, she vaulted 4.70 meters (15 feet, 5 inches). She won the USA Track and Field National Championships and her improvement for an elite vaulter out of college is estimated by Greg Hull, USA's Pole Vault Guru, to be double what the best U.S. women have ever done. I guess it does end up being a remarkable story after all.

Training partners Tori Pena, Nick Frawley, Kelsie Hendry, and Kylie.

Hmmm. Putting the past behind us. Perhaps, as per Kylie's lead and her successes, we should all give it a try, including me.

_____▲_____

Chapter 26

COMING OFF THE HILL

BOBBY DOUGLAS

"Anyone can stand tall on the high peaks. It is the people that survive the valleys between the peaks that will emerge the strongest. These survivors will be our leaders."

    -Preston Pearson

Bobby Douglas, an American legend.

Bobby Douglas was a five-time United States wrestling national champion. He served as the 1968 Olympic team captain, and was named the 1970 Outstanding Wrestler in the United States. He regularly beat Dan Gable, considered by many the most successful and well-known wrestler and coach in American history. Bobby later became a coach , and acted as head coach for the United States Olympic wrestling team in 1992 and 2004, and was a six-time assistant Olympic coach. He served as the national team coach in 1989, 1991, 2002 and 2003 and was the twelve-time Collegiate Conference coach of the year (three times at Iowa State University and nine times at Arizona State University). He wrote five books on wrestling, was inducted into the National Wrestling Hall of Fame and coached wrestler Cael Sanderson to a perfect 159-0 record, four NCAA National Championships and an Olympic gold medal.

    I worked with Bobby at Arizona State University from 1983 to 1993. I will never forget the talk he gave the team just two weeks before their trek to the 1988 National Collegiate Championships. Ever the scholar and always fascinated by history, he said, "If you ever studied Hannibal, you would know that Hannibal told his men that they need to be able to come off the mountain that they had climbed," --that success was more than just climbing. He told them that the part of the season that had gone by for his team had been the ascent -- the dual meets, the National Dual Championships, the PAC-10 Championships, and even all of the weight room workouts and torturous weekly runs up Squaw Peak. Now they had done all of the climbing they could do, and they needed to "come down off the mountain safely, effectively, and with the passion and enthusiasm they had climbed up with."

As a young coach, I never considered researching Hannibal, Sun Tzu, Genghis Khan, Caesar, Musashi, or Alexander The Great--leaders Bobby Douglas knew and quoted. I also never considered coming down off the hill and what he meant by that. In this case it meant plenty of rest, restorative techniques, mental visualization of performances, proper travel and just plain taking care. Indeed, there was more to success than just pushing harder all the time.

I look back about two decades later, older and at least somewhat wiser, and I appreciate Bobby's analogy and that he had drawn from history's great leaders to find that wisdom. The University of Iowa wrestling team, coached by Dan Gable—Bobby's competition—had unparalleled success at those NCAA Championships for the preceding ten consecutive years; they won the title every year, without fail. 1988 turned out different. The well-rounded Arizona State team, coached by scholar and theoretical tactician Bobby Douglas, pulled off the unthinkable by ending Iowa's reign as NCAA champions. That group of wrestlers did emerge victorious, as did I, in having the privilege to learn from a master, Bobby Douglas. That trip off the mountain was sweet.

Chapter 27

TAKING RISKS

JOHN VEHR

"The person who risks nothing, does nothing, has nothing, is nothing, and becomes nothing. He may avoid suffering and sorrow, but he simply cannot learn and feel and change and grow and love and live."
-Leo F. Buscaglia

John Vehr is a maverick. It's a title he wears well. He is also atypical, quirky, eccentric, outside the box, and downright quite fascinating at times. These are all charges he cannot and will not deny. While I'm calling him names, I have to throw out one equally descriptive adjective: risk taker.

Vehr owns Timney Triggers, which manufactures "the world's finest trigger." His company flourishes. Vehr lives on prestigious Camelback Mountain in Phoenix and owns a 37-acre ranch in Dewey, Arizona. He drives a Cobra when he isn't driving his custom-made Porsche, Audi or his pick-up truck. He buys the finest wines, wears the finest clothes and stays in the finest hotels. Many have referred to him as "lucky," but it wasn't luck that got him there. Vehr stuck his future out on the limb, several times over, and took risks most would not consider.

The first major risk he took professionally was to sell the lucrative landscaping company he founded. He did so in 1994 when the business was booming. He did that in order to go work for his parents at their tiny trigger manufacturing plant, a place he had never even visited. It was also a place that could not pay him well. By his own admission, his salary was now one-third of what it had been. Five years later, he was making only three-quarters of what he had previously made in landscaping. It was at this time he concocted the solution of buying the company from his parents. That way he felt he would generate more business and make more money. They passed on his offer.

Undaunted, Vehr came back to them again with an offer considerably more than the company was worth, not a seemingly bright business move. It was a huge risk that would put him in debt to the tune of a million dollars plus. He said he wanted to over pay because "they were my parents" and "money is everywhere so I figured I could make enough to do so." They took the offer this time. Sadly, and suddenly, his parents both passed away. John Vehr was now overpaying the heirs, not benefitting his parents and in debt over a million dollars while earning even less money annually.

"What can I say?" he says today about these risks. "I firmly believe one gets paid for his time, the more responsibility one has, the more he gets paid, but you only get rewarded for risking. More risk equals more reward."

It was at this time he completely shifted the way the company worked and he threw a great deal of his earnings back into the company. He again borrowed millions of dollars so he could purchase new equipment, pieces of equipment that to this day he has no idea how to operate or even turn on. He cut his staff size down by a third, preferring to keep only "astonishingly talented people." He pays those folks about twice as much as the industry norm. His company has become six times larger in only eleven years and he has established the standard of quality in the industry. It has been a fairy-tale success.

And about those amazing cars he drives? That isn't the goal at all. "What I learned from taking risks is the freedom to live life as I see fit, to do what seems important to me," he says. John donates in the six-figure range to charities annually.

Creating a new industry standard, owning a beautiful city home and ranch, driving sleek performance machines, paying people exceptionally well and donating hundreds of thousands for the betterment of others. Not bad for a guy who sold a lucrative business to work for a third of his salary. Apparently, there is something to be said for taking risks.

Chapter 28

ADVENTURISM
STEPHANIE MURATA

"The pool's open. Jump in."
  -Unknown Club Med Scuba Instructor

I met Stephanie Murata about two decades ago, when I was one of Arizona State University's strength and conditioning coaches. Steph was just starting to wrestle, something she had never done before. At the time, I was writing lifting programs for Trisha Saunders, the top female wrestler in the country, who was also mentoring Steph. She asked me if I would be willing to write her lifting programs as well. I told her, quite simply, "No."

I was in the midst of the off-season football-training program and so I had eighty guys who needed my attention in the weight room. I was shocked that Stephanie had burst into my work environment and asked a favor of someone she had never met before. Couldn't she see I was working, that I was getting paid to work with the football team and not any average Jane off the street who decided to take up athletics?

Steph went on her way and I went back to work, still amazed by the whirlwind that had popped in. That was twenty years ago, and to this day I still write Stephanie Murata's strength and conditioning programs. I'm not sure how it happened. I think about a month after our first meeting she came back and asked again, as if the first "no" had never happened. Maybe it was the third time she asked me. Apparently Stephanie was going to win this battle and her game plan was a principle of erosion. She would wear me down until she became a lifelong friend, someone I respect deeply, and a teacher.

My lesson from Stephanie is well summarized by this chapter's quote. Years ago, my wife Janet and I went scuba diving in the Bahamas. When we reached the dive site, far out in the ocean, the small Belgian scuba master looked at us and said, "The pool's open. Jump in."

Stephanie Murata jumped into wrestling. She won the National Championships nine times, and was named Outstanding Wrestler of the nation on multiple occasions. She competed in the World Championships many times and has seen most of the world as an international competitor. She had top American, Cuban and Russian coaches work with her and she trained with the top female and male competitors in the history of the sport.

Her adventurism is not restricted to a passion for freestyle wrestling. Stephanie earned her bachelor's degree in biology from the University of California Davis. For years she practiced Tae Kwon-do. She has competed in National Judo Championships. She plays the harp. She has helped deliver lambs and other farm animals at birth. She had surgery in Siberia, has had buttons sewn into her ears to help prevent cauliflower ear and has been the head coach of a woman's college wrestling program. She has lived in Florida, California, Arizona, Nevada, Oklahoma, Colorado, Iowa and others which I am sure have eluded my memory. She is now certified as a Physician's Assistant. She has also become as good a friend as anyone could ever have.

I think Stephanie has lived life the way we're supposed to. Life is a pool, and it is open. We should all jump in.

Chapter 29

THE GOAL IS THE PROCESS

SENSEI MARLON MOORE

"Victory in life is not acquiring a new technique, but developing spirit and mental attitude."
    -Unknown

Martial arts have always been steeped in myth and mysticism and are often associated with flashy kicks and showy self-defense maneuvers. But true martial arts, to me, should not be about those things. Martial arts should be about the development of character through austere training.

Judo, in particular, is not only an art that can be used to choke a man until he looses consciousness. Its literal translation is, "gentle way." The "do" in Judo means "way," and indeed, most traditional martial arts were formed for the explicit purpose of teaching a better way. The expressed purpose of judo is "the harmonious development and eventual perfection of the human character." Even though the training can be severe and the fighting is brutal, the purpose is for self-betterment.

Karate-do practitioners share on this path to find the way of betterment. Traditional Japanese dojo often require students to recite dojo kun, the expressed purposes of that style. Examples of dojo kun in dojos I have spent considerable time in, roughly translated, include: seek perfection of character, be faithful, respect others, refrain from violent behavior, cultivate a spirit of effort, live the way of truth, and perfect the mind of patience. Master Teruyuki Okazaki, one of the greatest karate masters of all time, said, "Karate is not just about developing incredible moves, amazing speed, and great strength. Karate is not just a system of self-defense. Karate is a way of life. Karate is a means toward the perfection of character."

In my time as a martial artist, I've seen a lot of karate and Chinese Kung Fu practitioners—even those with great technique—miss the point. I see many chasing trophies and inflated belt ranks. I've seen far too many practitioners award themselves unearned black belts or even high rank black belts, such as an eighth degree. I am thankful to have trained with instructors who taught me both martial arts techniques and what a martial artist should be. I trained in Marlon Moore's dojo for decades. Over the time I trained there, his thick brown hair has thinned and turned to gray. The quick punches have slowed a bit. Long bouts of intense fighting have shortened in duration, and many have been replaced with drills designed to enhance technical skill. Sensei has grown older and a bit slower, but his lessons have become more valuable with time. This Sensei taught me not to chase trophies and not to chase rank. In fact, I first earned a black belt rank eighteen years ago, and have not yet tested for the second-degree black belt. Yet Sensei doesn't chastise me for this. Instead, he says, "Tim, the goal is the process." I have come to realize if a martial arts student, athlete or even a student merely focuses on doing the process properly—giving their very best every day—the outcome will be favorable. There just isn't a need to worry about it, or give it any consideration. The whole trick is to do the process properly. The goal, therefore, is the process.

In my two decades of obsessive martial arts study, I have always found his words to ring true. I've seen the martial artists clamoring for attention, the self-promoters and the self-promoted, not to mention the eight-foot trophies that can be turned on like lamps. I see fewer true martial artists, martial artists who "get it." These are the people who perpetuate the meaning of the art. To me, a martial artist can achieve no higher honor than to truly understand the objectives of the Japanese martial arts. Sensei Marlon has helped me to be one of the ones to not only "get it," but to pass "it" along to others. Thank you, Sensei Marlon. My goal will always be that process.

Chapter 30

PERSPECTIVE

DREW BROWN

"Everything can be taken from man except the last of the human freedoms, his ability to choose his own attitude in any given set of circumstances, to choose his own way. Remember this choice of attitude when you are feeling overwhelmed by your circumstances."

-Victor Frankl

Drew Brown, a businessman I had the pleasure of training, graduated from Notre Dame Law School. He has a lovely wife, Laurie, and three outstanding children. He is a partner in the well-respected real estate development company DMB, with the "D" representing his name. Drew is a large component of DMB's superb reputation. Deeply intelligent, he often takes time to deliberate and provide thoughtful and meaningful guidance.

Many years ago, I was taking Drew through a particularly tough workout one day when I told him I was traveling to Florida to compete in the National Judo Championships. I commented that this meet would challenge me because I only had my brown belt at that time and would be competing against some of the country's top black belts. I had three years of experience to draw from, compared to twenty or more years of the high-level black belts.

"Tim, have you resigned yourself to having a good vacation in Florida after the tournament, regardless of the outcome?" Drew asked me.

"Drew, I'm not going to go frolicking all over Florida like a typical kid at Disney World if I get my butt kicked," I said, an admittedly high-testosterone response.

"Listen," he said. "We've already established that you're an underdog. You're a good athlete. You're an exceptionally hard worker. You are, however, giving up more than twenty years of experience and probably aren't the front-runner to win. That leaves you with one of two choices. You can spend the rest of your vacation time in Florida upset about something in the past that you cannot change, or you can give it your best, and if it doesn't work out that you beat everyone, you can move on and still have a good time."

I have to say he put things into perspective for me. I'm guessing Drew Brown has never done a martial arts workout in his life, but he hit me right between the eyes with the logic of an old sensei. He was right, of course. My objective should have been to give my very best in the competition and to grow from the experience. When that competition was over--win, lose, or draw--I needed to accept my fate, and live life to its fullest.

I have gone on to share Drew Brown's wisdom with hundreds of other athletes, to help them gain perspective on competition and how it fits into life. I now tell my athletes that if they performed phenomenally, they should enjoy it for twenty-four hours and then get back to reality. Any more time spent on reflecting back is wasted time. In the same way, an atrocious performance gets twenty-four hours of mourning and reflection. Any more time in this case is also wasted time. Regardless of the outcome, they need to go and live life to its fullest.

The martial arts advice I got from a non-martial artist was as good as any I have ever been given. But then again, if you knew Drew Brown, that wouldn't surprise you. My life has been enriched by his simple words of wisdom. Thank you, Drew Brown, for not only helping me, but for helping hundreds of others through me. May they always share your perspective.

Chapter 31

PERSPECTIVE

EZY RODRIGUEZ

"In my own life I've practiced stepping back a bit, emotionally, from difficult situations so that I could regain clarity of perspective. It's quite a miraculous feeling to recognize that we don't have to be victims of circumstance because the very freedom we seek is within each of us."

-Chelle Thompson, Editor of "Inspiration Line"

I stepped onto the mat for my last fight at the 2008 AAU National Karate Championships. I was amped up. I had to be. I received some seriously questionable calls by judges the previous year and I was coming back with a vengeance. Besides, the winner would be the National Champion. For me, that would be no easy task. Across from me stood Ezy Rodriguez of Florida. For several consecutive years Ezy either won this event or placed in the top three. The fact is, he is a better karate-ka than I am. He is a smart fighter, more talented, has better technique and trained with better partners than I. He's a much better person off the mat as well. More on that later.

During the match, we went back and forth in score. It was going to be tough to beat this guy, to solve this problem. Then I saw an opening. I fired a roundhouse kick to the left side of his ribcage. I buried it, deep. I was excited at feeling the hard contact and knew I had scored.

My elations turned out to be premature. He caught the kick with his left hand, trapped against his ribs. He just held it there—too long. My mind started racing.

They have to score that. It was too solid. Why aren't they stopping the fight and scoring the point? Did I miss the call? There are different rules in different organizations. Maybe they won't score it. Why aren't they stopping the fight? Why is this bastard hanging on to my leg so long and why aren't they stopping this? This guy is severely disrespecting me and they aren't stopping it. He's not going to disrespect me in this fight.

I did what comes naturally to many fighters, especially ones that are amped up and trying to win a National Championship. I drilled him in the face with my right hand—super hard. I may not be a smart man, or even a good one, but I am a hard-punching man and my right hand is nicknamed "comatose" for a reason.

Faster than you can say, "Tim is an idiot," Ezy's head whiplashed back, blood spewing from his nose. It took the paramedics several minutes to get it to stop. It was ugly, I was ugly. It was above and beyond what the rules allow. It wasn't Ezy's fault. He was waiting for the judges to stop the fight, as they should have. He was an unfortunate victim. I was, unfortunately, a moron.

After the fight, I went to greet Ezy. I wanted to apologize and ask for forgiveness. Being the amazing person he is, he shrugged it off, saying most fighters slip up in the heat of the battle. It humbled me even more. Then I mentioned that I had not seen him for two years, and asked him where he had been.

"Fighting cancer. I almost died," he replied. That hit me harder than I had hit him. Here was a man, a good man, no, a great man. He almost died from cancer and fought it hard for two years.

He was a gentleman. He was coming back to something he loved and something he thoroughly excelled at. He had a noble, just and healthy perspective. I had a moron's perspective.

Since then, I have seen Ezy Rodriguez several times and I pray that deep down in his heart he knows he is one of my heroes. I fought for a medal. He fought for his life. I fought outside of accepted rules. He fought adhering to them.

How could I not love Ezy Rodriguez today? He stood before me, bleeding and battered, but ready to fight on. He fought on, even though he had fought for two years straight, just to live. He taught me more in two minutes about perspective than I apparently learned in my lifetime. My perspective is now much clearer: I need to be more like Ezy Rodriguez. He is in my life to shine as an example for what a man should truly be and I hope someday to be in his ballpark…both as a person and a karate-ka.

Chapter 32

PERSPECTIVE

"GERONIMO"

"Champion the right to be yourself; dare to be different and to set your own pattern; live your own life and follow your own star."
-Wilfred Peterson

I have been afforded many opportunities in my life to gain an appropriate perspective, but quite honestly, I'm not the sharpest knife in the drawer. Drew Brown, Ezy Rodriquez and many others have been put in my life to help me because I apparently need a great deal of reinforcement to learn. Even dogs have tried.

It was a typical hot Phoenix summer Saturday. As usual, I went to the dojo to train for three grueling hours. I returned home utterly exhausted and mentally challenged by what I knew was coming up. The night before we had a huge wind and rainstorm drive through our acre of land, which is enveloped in eucalyptus trees. There were branches down everywhere and most were the size of regular trees. My wife Janet was out of town so I was going to have to be a solo lumberjack and I wanted to do a

great job to honor her so that she could return to a beautiful, happy home, free of hard-core labor.

Nine hours later, in the one hundred degree Phoenix heat, I had finished cutting, loading and unloading fourteen over-flowing pick-up truckloads of branches. My yard looked great again. I showered, iced my back and knee, took overdoses of vitamins and anti-inflammatories, ate and drank as much as I could and went to sleep. I awoke in the morning and went outside to admire my job well done. I was devastated.

Unbeknownst to me, another micro-burst had gone through my property when I slept. It looked like a war had been waged in my once spotless yard. I could not have gotten angrier. I stormed out into the yard full of anger, disappointment, pity and about every other negative emotion a man can experience. I stared at the branches with disbelief. It seemed like an eternity.

That feeling was snapped out of me the way limbs were snapped off the trees hours earlier when our chocolate Labrador retriever Geronimo sprinted past me, grabbed a huge branch and took off through the yard. She started bucking like a rodeo bull apparently unable to restrain her enthusiasm. What on earth is that stupid dog doing with that stupid branch, I wondered.

Just then, she dropped it. Then she rolled over, got up and bucked some more. She re-grabbed it and took off, bucking again. Another drop. Another roll-over. More bucking. It was bliss for her and then it hit me. Those branches were down whether or not the dog and the man were happy about it or upset. The dog that I thought was stupid was happy. The owner (me) that the dog knew was stupid was not happy. Same event. One had bliss, one a nightmare.

90

I surrendered my feelings of anger and self-pity and became more like Geronimo that day. I learned to embrace life and to not carry around those burdens we choose to carry, such as resentment, self-pity, disappointment. Granted, those six truckloads of branches I cut, loaded and unloaded that day, did not make me buck, sprint or roll-over, but I had gained a very powerful perspective that I still hold (most of the time) today.

May we all have a little more Geronimo in us and a little less "us" in us.

Chapter 33

EXTENDING YOUR FAMILY

CASANOVA BROTHERS

"'Ohana' means family - no one gets left behind, and no one is ever forgotten."

    -Chris Sanders and Dean DeBlois, *Lilo & Stitch*

Mike (left) and Tony Casanova (right) with Luigi (center).

Having grown up in eastern Pennsylvania, I was exposed to many great pizza options. There were lots of "mom and pop" pizzerias and they were all good. Arizona is another story. I've lived here for over twenty-five years, tried dozens of pizza places and have hated them all, including all of the ones that claimed to have New York pizza. Actually, I especially grew bitter towards them because they got my hopes up and then became a bigger disappointment. The only exception was Patsy Grimaldi's. Their pizza was excellent—actually, it was better than that, it was superb, but it was drastically different than what I grew up, so I was still left lingering for what I once had.

Our close friends, the Copes, are Arizonans originally from New Jersey and they suggested we try Casanova Brothers. We didn't. After 25 years, I was tired of the disappointment and the place Casanova Brothers had moved into was previously a pizza place with awful pizza. It wasn't until years later that my wife Janet and I would venture into Casanova Brothers.

I knew this place was the real deal when we opened the door. Some guy from behind the counter whom I didn't know yells, "Hey! How are you guys doing?" He acted as though he was a relative. I started trying to figure out if I had met this guy before.

We proceeded to place our order without high expectations and sat down. A few minutes later our pizza arrived. It floored me. It was indeed the real deal. Finally, after 25 years, I found a great slice of pizza that I could order by the slice. Honestly, it felt like I found the Loch Ness Monster or Sasquatch.

"Janet, this is so good."

"I agree," she replied. "I can't believe it."

"I'm going to find out why they can do it and no one else out here can."

"What are you going to do?" she asked, giving me the Janet eyes that let me know I'm onto yet one more of my bad ideas.

"I'm asking the loud guy. He seemed like he will chat with me."

"Tim, no."

"Hey! Pal, come over here and sit down with us for a minute, will you?" I blurted out across the seating area. When he came over and sat down, I went into my tirade.

"I've lived in Arizona for 25 years and the pizza sucks. Why is yours different?" I inquired.

"Tony" then explained to me they have a hired chef, they make their own sauce, the flour most places use costs eight dollars per bag but they spend forty-two dollars on much better flour. It all made sense. This guy then sat with us, still treating us like family, for twenty-five minutes. This guy was so nice, so comfortable, and so sincere and intent on what we were saying it shocked me.

A month later, we went back.

"Hey Tim and Janet. Welcome back!" It was Tony again—Tony Casanova, the owner. The sincere interest he showed in us was the real deal—just like his pizza. To further surprise, I noticed how he seemed to personally know every customer's name. So did his brother Mike and the customer service machine Luigi. It has been years now since Janet and I first went in there and have always been greeted with a hug and a loud New York, "Hey!" All of the customers talk to each other and you quite often see the same people there week after week. The food is that good (all of it, not just the pizza) and the atmosphere is unparalleled. Needless to say, we have referred dozens of people there. Of course, the second time they open that door they are greeted with, "Hey," followed by their first names.

The Casanova Brothers goal isn't about just making pizzas and making money. Others might be focused only on improving profits by purchasing cheaper ingredients, but the Casanova Brothers' goal is to make one giant, happy family. They do this so well I swear I'd be a regular forever, even if their pizza hadn't been so superior. It's impossible to walk out of that place without a smile because I know my extended family there will cook for me and serve me as such.

Seeing this different approach is a lesson in itself, and one from which I want to tell my extended family, "Hey! Thank you for your love. I love you guys too." I guess you do reap what you sow.

▲

Chapter 34

MAKING PEOPLE FEEL SPECIAL
BRETT PREACH

"I've learned that people will forget what you said, people will forget what you did, but people will never forget how you made them feel."
    -Dawn Cassaday

Brett Preach basking in the love of his family.

I was honored in my previous book to write about my own father when it came to parenting. My father was a very caring, loving parent. And even though he has been in heaven for 26 years now I carry his lesson with me every day.

I am also honored to write about another parent and his loving and caring style. His name is Brett Preach.

Several years ago I had the pleasure of training all four of Brett's daughters. All four girls were stand-out players at Xavier College Preparatory and, believe it or not, all ended up playing on State Championship teams.

One day when I had all four girls in, I asked the oldest one, Lindsay, "hey, which one of you is daddy's girl?"

Without hesitation she replied, "I am".

A few minutes later I went to her younger sister second sibling Kristen and asked her the same question. I got the same response-the exact same response ver batim.

Now I was flat out amusing myself and you can guess what I did next. I went to daughter number three, Lacey. She gave me the exact same reply. I was now headed for home plate. There was only one left, the youngest daughter Stephanie.

"Hey Steph, which one of you is daddy's girl?"

"Tim, come on Tim" she said with her usual overabundance of enthusiasm, "you know I am".

Four daughters, all so different. Yet, all four instantly blurted out that they were daddy's girl. All four truly believed it. Any man that can pull that off is indeed a superior parent and worthy of our attention. Perhaps we can all strive a little harder to make others in our lives feel as special as Brett Preach made all of his daughters feel.

Chapter 35

FOLLOWING THROUGH

ANN FREDERICK

"Until intelligence is linked with appropriate action and followed through, there is no real accomplishment."
  -Unknown

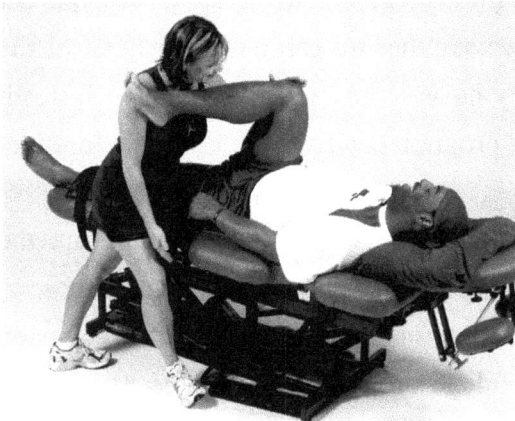

The best stretching the best: Ann Frederick and Donovan McNabb.

Ann Frederick has made a career out of stretching people. She and her husband, Chris, operate a business called Stretch to Win. Her clients are largely professional athletes. Many of those athletes feel she is the best in the world at what she does. I echo the sentiment. Literally and figuratively, Ann Frederick and her husband wrote the book on stretching. The text, entitled *Stretch to Win*, is the industry standard. I have never had reservations about sending the elite athletes I train to Ann. She matches skill with caring, and clients are invariably thrilled with her. On my end, the players I send to her can work out longer and harder in my program, and are less likely to be injured.

What most of my clients don't think about is that it hasn't always been that way. Once upon a time, Ann Frederick was not, to be politically correct, quite as wonderful as she is now.

I met Ann in the early 1990s while I was serving as head strength and conditioning coach at Arizona State University. She called me to ask if I would talk to her about getting involved with the athletic department. She mentioned she had been teaching some stretch classes at a local fitness facility and that she had a lifetime experience in dance; she seemed enthusiastic and pleasant. I didn't think we could create an opening for her in the program, but figured I would try to help her the way that former strength coach Don Clemons had helped me when I wanted to get into the collegiate athletic arena. His one act made my career take off. In sports, we say that we can never repay all of the effort our predecessors gave us. They have simply given too much. Instead, we try to pay forward to others so the program can live on. With that in mind, I met Ann.

A few days after we met, she offered to stretch me. Simply put, the stretching was not what I felt it needed to be. I found out she had no degree in any related field, and no certification in any related field. Tactfully, I suggested to Ann she needed to check into a college program and thanked her for her effort. She was exceptionally nice about it. We parted, and I assumed our paths would not meet again.

Ann called me a few months later, to my surprise. She told me she had toned down the intensity of the stretching and that she planned to finish her college degree. She wanted to meet again, and she seemed so sincere that I agreed. The second stretching session actually felt better. We met a third time, a fourth, and then a fifth. At that point, I started to notice characteristics of Ann Frederick that made her stand out. Her stretching improved and her passion was obvious. She loved doing this and would make it work, regardless of the time and effort required.

A few years later, Art Martori, founder of the Sunkist Kids Wrestling Club, asked me to provide strength and conditioning services to the elite wrestlers he had moved to Phoenix in preparation for the 1996 Olympic trials and games. By then, Ann had become pretty good, and was asked to provide stretching services to the group. We did so in Phoenix for six months before traveling to the first of the pre-Olympic training camps. At the camp, Ann and I spent three hours a night discussing stretching and all other aspects of training. In the past, I had instructed her, but things had changed. Ann was finishing her degree at Arizona State University and become a compulsive student. She worked with top physiologists, biomechanists and lab researchers at ASU and throughout the country. She volunteered time with every athlete she could. She did a one-year graduate assistantship in the ASU athletic department with Rich Wenner, the strength coach who succeeded me. She taught me. It was awesome to see how she grew.

Over a decade has passed since Ann, who had nothing but desire, began pursuing her dream and started private practice. She went to the Atlanta Olympic Games and has been flown all over the country by professional athletes for her expertise. She stretched athletes at three Super Bowls. She and Chris completed a DVD of their Stretch to Win methods and wrote a definitive guide on how athletes should stretch. Ann is a true example of someone who went from the proverbial outhouse to the penthouse.

Ann, thank you for all the times you have stretched me and for taking care of the athletes I have referred you. Thank you for the friendship and the lesson about following through. You deserve all the wonderful experiences and accolades you have earned. May your passion live on forever.

Chapter 36

DELIBERATELY INSPIRING

DON ROBINSON

"In dealing with persons as intractable and as difficult to influence as a pig or a fish, the whole secret of success depends on finding the right approach."
-I Ching

In my thirteen years at Arizona State University, I handled the off-court and off-field strength and conditioning programs for twenty-six varsity teams. These ranged from National Collegiate Athletic Association national team champions in archery, badminton, gymnastics and wrestling, to other teams struggling to gain a spot in the national top twenty.

In that time, I worked with a lot of coaches. Football alone had four head coaches, each with nine full-time assistants and another six or so graduate or volunteer assistants. All totaled, I probably worked with over fifty coaches on the football staff alone. Add that to the head coaches and assistants for twenty-five other sports, and I'm sure I must have interacted with at least two hundred of them.

Each coach had their own style, code of conduct and expectations. At that time, Arizona State University ranked among the top ten athletic departments and so I had the sense I was working with some of the best. A few of those coaches stood out for me: Bobby Douglas, the wrestling coach, and Debbie Brown, the volleyball coach. Each had amazing athletic careers themselves and became effective coaches. Their athletes improved tremendously, their teams met with success and their athletes loved them. The other superstar was gymnastic coach Don Robinson.

Don did it all. Don coached the NCAA National Team Champion, in a state whose high school recruiting base barely existed. He coached dozens of individuals to National Championships during a span of twenty-five years. He took athletes all over the world to compete and to succeed in competition.

His coaching style involved cultivating a sort of family. A lot of sports teams try this, but unlike most others, Don pulled it off. Over twenty years later, members of his team still feel like family. The rings we received as staff from the NCAA Championship team have "family" engraved on them. Don Robinson did his job and did it well. He was so sincere about unity that he hoped to unite the entire athletic department as gymnastics family. He walked all six floors of the athletic complex each day and handed each and every employee—from the Director of Athletics to the volunteer student employee—an inspiring message. Often the quotes came from the Edge Learning Institute. Other times they were pertinent quotes he typed and photocopied. They were all motivational. One of his quotes: "Everything can be taken from man except the last of the human freedoms, his ability to choose his own attitude in any given set of circumstances, to choose his own way. Remember this choice of attitude when you are feeling overwhelmed by your circumstances," described Don and his feelings.

I heard people in the athletic department say Don often spent an hour every day attempting to inspire others. That means he must have spent five hours per typical week, about two-hundred-and-fifty hours a year and over five thousand hours in his career inspiring others. That is the equivalent of over two years worth of time he spent helping others try to achieve higher standards.

Don Robinson went above and beyond. He didn't need to provide quotes and words of wisdom to every person in the athletic department, but he did anyway. Sadly, the gymnastics program was eventually shut down. They may have taken the gymnastics program out of the university and out of the NCAA, but they can never take Don Robinson out of our hearts. He and his efforts to inspire others will remain with us always.

Today "Coach" Robinson is in heaven and I'll bet he's passing on those uplifting and inspiring messages to others.

Chapter 37

SHOWING BELIEF

FRED MILLER

"One person with a belief is equal to a force of ninety-nine who have only interests."

-John Stuart Mill

I graduated college in 1982 and then moved from Pennsylvania to Arizona to pursue a career as an entry-level strength and conditioning coach. I started volunteering at Arizona State University's athletic department and was particularly grateful to be working under the guidance of strength coach Don Clemons. Being passionate, I worked hard for Don. Since Arizona State University wasn't paying me anything, I had to find a part-time job. At one point, Don told me that if I got accepted into a graduate program, he could get me a graduate assistant stipend through the athletic department. I could not have been happier. I had graduated with my bachelor's degree with honors and loved academia. I had the opportunity to get my master's degree work paid for, to get a stipend and to be upgraded from volunteer assistant to graduate assistant in a fantastic athletic program. Life was going exactly according to my dreams.

I applied to the Master of Science program in Physical Education and started taking classes. I was asked to take the GRE exam and was told I needed to meet the 500 point mark in both math and english. I fell short, scoring 490 and 480, respectively. Meanwhile, I had earned A's in the first two classes toward my program of study. Despite the A's, I would not be accepted into the program. The chair of the department I applied to told me that because

I had scored below 500 in english, I probably would not have the ability to properly write a thesis. I told him I had been published thirteen times as an undergraduate, but was told that was not representative of my writing ability. I had to take the exam a second time. I'm not sure how the predicative value of a test we know has flaws tells us a man who had written thirteen magazine articles as an undergraduate can't write well enough, but that's what I was told. I had to re-take the GRE exam.

Again, I scored 490 and 480 respectively. By then I had twelve credits, 4 classes completed, all A's. Consistent as I was in my test scores, I at least was also consistent in my grades. Still the department of physical education denied me admission. I took the exam a third time--and scored 490 and 480 again. By then I had added another few classes, scored A's, and was denied admission a third time. Two of the six classes I had were with Fred Miller, the former ASU Athletic Director, who had designed virtually all of ASU's athletics facilities. He was a visionary and an excellent professor and mentor to me. I met with him about my dilemma. I told him I had completed my 18th unit (Master's candidates need 24 total units and a thesis to graduate.) I told him I had a perfect 4.0 grade point average but was thinking of dropping out, he told me, "You wait right here until I am back."

I sat in his small hot office, staring at a nauseating shade of green paint, for almost three hours that day, certain that he had gone somewhere and forgotten me. I was no longer living the dream. In that rickety uncomfortable wood chair, my back was killing me and I was sure I should have left hours earlier. I hung in simply because I had believed so much in him.

He finally returned. He had personally gone to every person on the admissions board and explained to them why they should admit me. He talked about the two A's I got in his classes, that I had outscored all of the students in both classes, and that I had written a hundred-and-four page paper on weight room facility design. That paper, he said, should far outweigh the predictive capability of a standardized exam. Needless to say, only through Fred Miller did I gain acceptance into the Master of Science program in physical education at Arizona State University. Only through Fred Miller was I able to graduate with a perfect 4.0 grade point average in that program of study.

Fred Miller believed in a passionate and hardworking—if not naïve— kid from the cornfields of Pennsylvania. If he hadn't, I probably would have dropped out and not achieved my academic goal. I've often thought that it does no good to care about someone without letting them know. I've also thought there are many ways to show that you care. By showing his belief in me, Fred Miller showed that he cared for me. Though I have not seen him in more than twenty years, that one act of caring taught me to care more for and believe in others, and I'll deeply appreciate him forever. Now that's a real professor.

Chapter 38

VERSATILITY

FRED WAKEFIELD

"Great men blaze new trails, where there is less traffic, but more promise."
    -Gary B. Wright

Jim Steiner called me on behalf of his agency, SFX, in 2000. Jim represented Jerry Rice and a whole lot of other NFL superstars, and wanted me to help him prepare his new signees for the 2000 NFL Scouting Combine. We hammered out details pretty quickly and I was pleased when Jim and his associates Ben Dogra and Mark Heligman recruited a solid group. They signed future first round picks Deuce McAlister and Justin Smith, as well as standouts Chris Chambers, Torrance Marshall, Jared Cooper, and Jabari Holloway. The players had good work ethics and a great deal of natural talent.

Fred, the beast, with All-Conference runner, Julie Fisher.

The dark horse of the group was a defensive end from the University of Illinois, Fred Wakefield. As a 6'7" and 278 pound lineman, Fred enjoyed a good, but not standout, senior year. He was a marvelous athlete though, playing football and basketball, and running track at a high school a few hours away from Chicago. Given his overall athleticism, I was surprised to hear pre-draft predictions that he might be taken as late as the sixth or seventh round. Needless to say, Fred didn't like that prediction either.

Fred followed my lead and trained about as hard as someone can train for two months. His weight soared up to 290 pounds and he knocked two tenths of a second off his 40-yard dash. He ran all drills faster, and lifted more weight than ever in his life. He underwent an amazing transformation, one that would surely help him get drafted higher.

To my surprise, Fred not only wasn't selected higher, he wasn't selected at all. I'm not sure how this happened—it defied common sense. He later had to sign a free agent contract with the Arizona Cardinals. Interestingly enough, despite being a non-drafted rookie, Fred earned a starting job for most of his rookie season. He went from an un-drafted defensive end to a starting defensive end.

Time has a way of changing things, and soon enough Fred found himself moved from defensive end to a defensive tackle position. Again, only a minor contributing role was expected of him. Again, he earned a starting position.

After that season, the front office of the Cardinals decided to make a head coaching change and hired Denny Green. Denny came in with guns blazing and turned the whole place upside down. Amongst his changes, he tried to move Fred from the defensive line to the offensive line. This move rarely works, since the skill set differs so drastically. Often it is the kiss of death to a player's career; the player loses time he could be practicing defense and cannot keep up with offense.

Fred, being Mr. Versatile, pulled it off again, and earned starting jobs throughout the next season at both guard positions and both tackle positions. To make this happen, Fred often trained in the weight room twice a day and followed the strictest of dietary protocols designed by the top guy in the field, Tom Incledon. His weight increased from 295 to 325 pounds and he looked leaner than ever. His bench press went from 445 to 500 pounds and he showed no loss in foot speed. Fred's was truly an amazing transformation. Watching him train and play, I thought that he'd finally found his home, a home where he could blossom into one of the top players in the league.

The following year, 2006, Fred reached 330 pounds and peak condition. The staff coaches claimed that his performance was outstanding. Then, out of the blue, the tight-ends coach approached him on the practice field and asked Fred to join them in their pre-practice position meeting.

"Pretty cool," Fred thought. "They probably want me lined up as a tight-end to block on goal line situations," he later said to me. Little did he know, Denny Green had decided to take this phenomenal athlete, now a beast of a man, and move him outright to another new position, tight-end. Lo and behold, by the end of the season, Fred Wakefield found himself in a familiar role: an NFL starter in a new position.

Defensive end, defensive tackle, offensive guard, offensive tackle, tight-end. Fred re-invented himself over and over and each time produced winning results. Playing in the NFL is the dream of most every boy. Actually making it there is a rarity. Earning a job as a starter is one very few ever accomplish. Doing it over and over again as Fred Wakefield did…well, being a part of that and learning from it is priceless. I am proud to have been with Fred, training him, throughout the entire process.

Regardless of the need, Fred Wakefield found a formula to meet the challenge and crush it. His unyielding efforts, involving intense workouts, extra massage therapy sessions, stretching with Ann Frederick, and a strict supplement/nutritional program, paid off. Fred eventually retired, and started a career in business. I wouldn't be surprised to find him the next Wall Street guru. He is that versatile.

Chapter 39

MOVING ON TO BIGGER AND BETTER THINGS

JIM COPE

"You can't steal second base if you are afraid to leave first."
    -Unknown

In college, Dr. Frank Pullo, a professor of mine, told me a story. Frank was a lifetime fixture at East Stroudsburg State College, now East Stroudsburg University. During his tenure, he was the department head for the Physical Education and Exercise Physiology Department. He also ran the field house and facilities, was chairman of the intramurals and served as a teaching professor. During one of his classes he told us about a survey among athletes. The survey question asked, "If you could take a substance and were guaranteed to win an Olympic gold medal, but would die ten years later, would you do it?" According to Dr. Pullo, over 85% of all athletes answered "yes."

As a young competitive powerlifter, I probably would have answered the same way. I am pretty confident that my closest training partners, Joe Catalfamo, Todd VanBodegom-Smith, and Mark Shelhamer would have answered the same. The most fired up lifter of our group, Jim Cope, was a sure bet in my mind. To "Cope," as he was known, life consisted of three things: heavy squats, heavy bench presses and heavy dead lifts.

Cope was quite the lifter. At 165 pounds, having never taken a strength-inducing drug, he was destined for greatness. In national-level competition, with the strictest of judges and old-fashioned gear that isn't supportive like the gear today's powerlifters use, Jim squatted 622 pounds, bench pressed 363 pounds, dead lifted 633 pounds and posted a overall best meet total of 1598. The dead lift and total were recognized as all-time Junior World Records (for lifters under twenty-three years old). He did not surprise me by winning the Junior World Championships, in India, in a weight class higher than his normal limit. Jim Cope was good enough to beat the rest of the world in his weight class and the next highest weight class. He lived, breathed, and dreamt about powerlifting and it showed.

Because of powerlifting, Jim moved from his home in New Jersey to Phoenix. He wanted good training partners, like National Champions Rich Wenner, Kevin Dittler, Shannon Pratt, Chris Boillot and Bill Wong. He also wanted the direct coaching I could provide, and we set out to conquer the powerlifting world.

A short time after that, Jim's old high school and college football injuries started to catch up with him. Jim had blown out his knee in his college days, and the injury required the removal of his medial and lateral menisci, which are the two pads that act as shock absorbers or cushions between the upper and lower leg bones. To compound matters, he needed a reconstruction of his anterior cruciate ligament (ACL). After the initial surgery, he did considerably more damage when he returned to football. Though the powerlifting kept him structurally strong, it could not repair the huge amount of damage already done. He had to have radical surgery, and had fifteen bone chips removed from his knee. His career was over.

To this day, I am disappointed that Jim Cope could not live out the rest of his career. My coaching has gotten better with age, and I do think that with his passion and my coaching, he would have been unbeatable. I carried this thought for decades and every time I see the Junior World certificates in his den, I feel unsettled. I honestly believe he had a shot to beat all of the competitive lifters who were using steroids without ever touching the drugs himself.

Interestingly, Jim seems to have handled this better than I have. He continued his position with the Phoenix Police Department and was promoted to the rank of Sergeant. He has been a superstar in the department, according to the officers who work with him. He has also maintained a happy marriage with his wife, Jamie, and they have two wonderful daughters, Brittney and Carley. He has helped dozens of energetic go-getters find employment with the police department. He has won awards for his work and is a reliable friend.

Jim Cope never looked back, though he was the best in the world and had good reason to. He never questioned, complained or cried. He just moved forward with determination.

Once upon a time I was sure, of all the athletes I knew, Jim Cope would be the first to give up his life for an Olympic medal. Now I know why he was never in that position. He was destined to be greater at other things, and his ability to look forward enabled him to be a superb officer, husband, father and friend.

▲

Chapter 40

THE SURE BET

DR. MICHAEL LEE

"Stick with a winner."
   -John Jones

Michael Lee is an orthopedic surgeon who has served as head medical council to both the Arizona Diamondbacks in Major League Baseball and the Arizona Cardinals of the National Football League. During the past three decades, I've interacted with a lot of injured athletes, such as martial artists, Olympic and professional champions and the regular Joes of the world who ask me for a referral to a great doctor. I've also met with many medical doctors, especially orthopedic surgeons. Michael is one of the best. The superstar athletes trust him to repair their injuries and resurrect their careers.

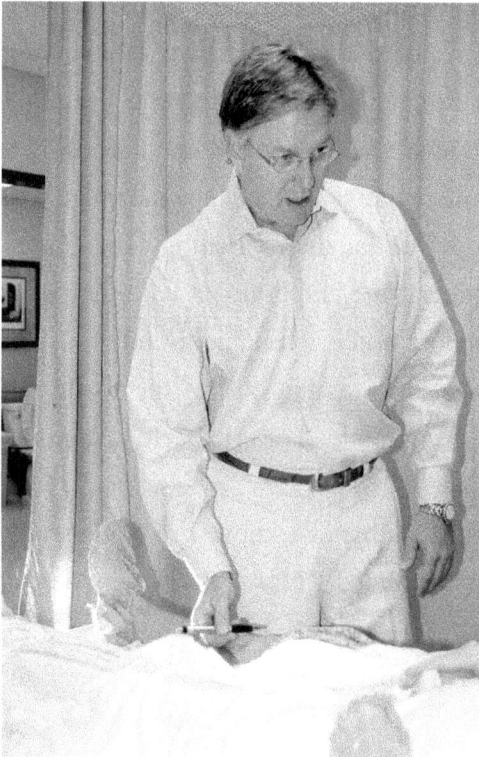

Time and time again, he has handled even the trickiest surgeries with skill and great results. I see his patients start physical therapy soon after his surgeries and they always do well. The best of the best trust him. He has a calm demeanor and never seems rushed, as so many doctors do. I once asked him six pages of written questions, literally, when he was treating me. He patiently went through each and every one, taking the time to thoroughly answer each question in great medical detail. He can make explanations as technical as necessary or put everything into layman's terms. Perhaps most important though, Dr. Michael Lee—in spite of his reputation for being the esteemed orthopedic surgeon of superstars---has always been polite, caring, fun and real. He has no air of pretentiousness, and no youth or professional athlete I have ever sent to him for his expert medical opinion has ever felt differently. Everyone comes away happy. As my friend Penny, an esteemed physical therapist said, "that guy is a sure bet."

Dr. Lee, thank you for all of the great work you have done for Janet and me, for being a guaranteed hit with the clients I have sent to you, for being a great guy and a great surgeon. I know everyone I send you in the future will say the same thing the others I've sent you have said for over a decade: "that guy is the best."

▲

Chapter 41

CONNECTING

DENISE DECKER

"The simple reality is most any level of lasting achievement takes effort. Often it means going above and beyond the call of duty."
-John Hinds

Denise Decker is my beloved friend. She owns and operates a business called Little Devils Gymnastics, a take-off from her time as an Arizona State Sun Devil gymnast. She teaches approximately eight hundred kids per year, ages three to twelve. She has done this exceptionally well for twenty-six years. It's not hard to figure out -- she has touched a lot of lives and knows a lot of people. The running joke is that she knows everyone in Phoenix and everything going on in their lives. That's not true. There are some new people moving in she hasn't yet met. Give her a few weeks though, and she'll get there. She simply lives to help her Little Devils gymnasts and their parents.

Denise could do a great job, collect her money and go home at the end of the day. She'd never just do that though --stopping at what others do – because Denise Decker shepherds all of us. She makes time for us, lifts us up, and helps us. She is a connector, a facilitator. She knows everyone's strengths and puts each in a position to help one another. To date, she has referred me clients, gotten me free parking passes to a boxing match, scheduled my wife and friends for various medical appointments because she knew the docs and could get us in faster, gotten jobs for my friends, taught gymnastics to my friend's children and too many others non-related things to remember.

I think anyone who knows her will say she shines as a light for us as to how we should help each other. After working so hard in her job and putting forth so much to make sure her gymnastics program is nothing short of amazing, she could go home and relax, knowing she has changed hundreds of lives. I am so thankful she doesn't do that. I'm pretty sure I speak for everyone in Phoenix to be grateful for her example.

Chapter 42

USING THE LEARNED LESSONS

RAY ARVIZU SR.

"If there's a will, there's a way."
   -Unknown

Ray Arvizu Sr. grew up with loving parents in a small Hispanic household in South Phoenix. His father worked hard and managed every dime to help keep the family afloat. It was a huge undertaking to make all ends meet. During those early years in South Phoenix, Ray Sr. fell in love with sports. He wasn't privileged to afford the private lessons required for golf or tennis. He didn't have the money to buy ice time for hockey. Basketball was another story. Hoops were available for free and Ray Sr. took to basketball; it became his love.

Years later, because of the combination of his extreme passion and excessive work ethic over thousands of hours of intense practice, Ray Sr. led Grand Canyon University to the NAIA National Championship. He followed up this success with a professional career in Mexico. Several years after that, he wed his sweetheart, Ernestina, and they started a family. Ray Sr. retired from the constant demands of traveling all over Mexico and went on to work for little pay for various companies in Arizona. He worked so hard that eventually Coca Cola offered him a job in marketing, a job that required him to move to Atlanta, Georgia. Unfortunately, this job too would provide him with a salary that would barely make ends meet. Ray Sr. had been down the road of hardship before; his childhood afforded him few luxuries. He had achieved great success in basketball, but only by outworking others, consistently.

He worked hard and into the early hours of the morning with Coca Cola, seizing every opportunity to learn about customer relations, sales and advertising. He sacrificed immediate gratification for a better long-term future, a lesson he had learned in his basketball playing days, when he had sacrificed the parties, beer drinking, and fun, to shoot baskets by himself on a 105 degree playground.

Ray Sr. and Ernestina then moved back to Arizona, borrowed what was a lot of money for them from a bank, and started their own advertising agency, Arvizu Advertising. As per usual, Ray Sr. started with nothing, but by working longer and harder than others, he created a huge success--the largest Hispanic-based advertising and promotions company in the United States.

Since formation of Arvizu Advertising and Promotions, Ray Sr. and Ernestina have raised and donated more than a million dollars for various charities and agencies, including churches, scholarship funds and tsunami relief. More astounding, they did this with four children of their own--and an additional two non-related boys, who they invited into their home to receive the benefits of a healthy, strong, stable existence. For these boys, the Arvizus pay food costs year round, sponsor club basketball participation and help them to become outstanding members of the community.

Ray Arvizu Sr. never set out to become ultra rich. In his own words, he simply applied the principles he learned in competitive basketball at a young age to his life and his business. In applying his life's lessons with a determined attitude and work ethic, he has been in a position to change many lives. We all have lessons presented to us. Sometimes we actually learn from them and utilize them to our benefit. It is my hope everyone who reads this book recognizes their life lessons and uses them to their benefit, as Ray Arvizu has his entire life.

▲

Chapter 43

HONESTY

TRISTAN BLALOCK

"An honest man is the noblest work of God."
   -Alexander Pope

In the sporting world, I often hear, "Practice makes perfect." Good coaches know this is not necessarily true. Practice can ruin athletes. If athletes perform movements incorrectly over and over again, athletes will get perfectly good at doing the wrong thing. Good coaches know that "practice makes permanent, not perfect." Only perfect practice makes perfect.

When I condition athletes, I often use hurdles, mini-hurdles, bags, cones and speed ladders. To encourage perfect practice, I have implemented a deterrent to keep athletes from hitting aforementioned training apparatus: push-ups.

One Tuesday about seven years ago, I had a 1:00 P.M. appointment with standout high school baseball player Tristan Blalock. He was one of those well-built guys who looked me in the eye and followed my coaching orders to

perfection. I had left the gym at 12:15 for a lunch, planning to grab a sub from Subway and be back by 12:45, fifteen minutes before Tristan was due.

When I got back with my sub, I was amazed to find what would normally be a very busy weight room empty, not a soul to be found anywhere. I sat to eat and out of the corner of my eye, saw atypical movements from behind a machine. What I saw floored me. I saw Tristan Blalock doing push-ups.

"Tristan, what are you doing?"

"Push-ups, Coach. I'm sorry I hit the ladder. I won't do it again," he said.

Apparently Tristan had beaten me back the weight room and started his warm-ups without me there, because he knew it was the right thing to do. According to his confession, he had hit the ladder and he gave himself push-ups. No one in the world except for Tristan Blalock would have ever known he hit the ladder in an empty room fifteen minutes before his workout was scheduled to start. Despite his probable chance of getting away with hitting the ladder, he knew what was the correct thing to do. He disciplined himself, so that he would be his very best. It was an act I just cannot fathom many athletes doing -- taking a penalty even though no one else witnessed the error. It was truly a one in a million experience to see.

Thank you, Tristan, for your honesty and for the lesson of how we all should be.

Chapter 44

ONE WELL-DEVELOPED SKILL

J.J. JANSEN

"Impossibility: a word only to be found in the dictionary of fools."
  -Napoleon Bonaparte

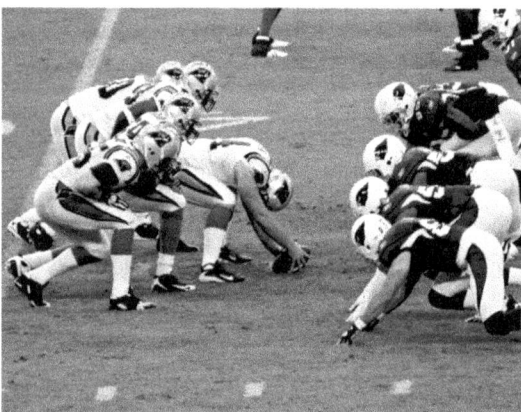
J.J. Jansen snapping in a game versus the Arizona Cardinals.

J. J. Jansen played some high school sports. He shared time as a first baseman on his high school team, a team that never achieved great success. Several players on that team got offers to play college baseball, but J.J. wasn't one of them. He also played a little football. When I say a little football, I mean just a little. In high school, he wasn't talented enough to be a stand-out on either the offensive or defensive side of the ball. J.J. was primarily recognized as a special teams player. He left high school as an average football player who played decent baseball, but had no college scholarship offers in either sport. Essentially all he had was desire to be a great long snapper.

The long snapper "hikes" or "snaps" the football to the punter or field goal holder on fourth downs. This is a very difficult skill and the slightest error can change the complexion of a whole game. The snap has to be fast, with a tight spiral of the ball, and in perfect position for the punter or holder to catch. Often the long snapper has his head down to view the target he is snapping to, and he is usually then assaulted by bigger, faster, stronger players. J.J. had a dream. He wanted to long snap at Notre Dame. Thee Notre Dame.

So J.J. walked on to the Notre Dame football program and during his freshman year, he watched a lot of Notre Dame football from the sidelines. Undaunted, he trained harder than ever and he snapped thousands of footballs, often to his retired engineer father, Rick. With each snap, he got better. Yes, this sounds like the start of a comparison to the movie, *Rudy*.

J.J.'s sophomore year, Notre Dame hired Charlie Weis as their new football coach. By then J.J. was the best snapper in the Notre Dame program. He got his first start in the most heralded Notre Dame game in many years, a nationally televised game against the number one ranked USC Trojans. His snapping skills were so sharp by that time he handled the incredible pressure of the game as though he had been doing it all of his life. From that point on, the job was his to keep.

J.J. never lost that starting job, and snapped over 300 balls in his career at Notre Dame. It is indeed a *Rudy*-like story…only J.J. was much more successful than Rudy ever dreamed of

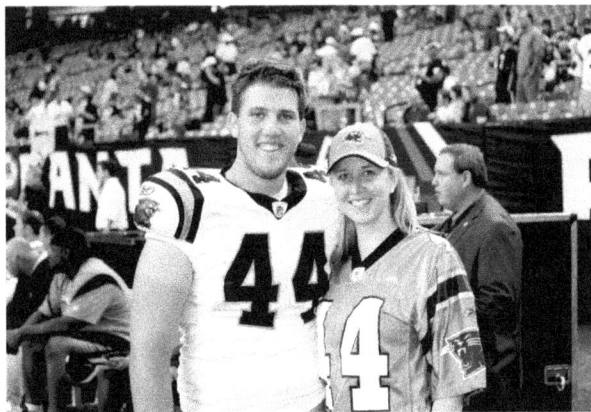

J.J.'s biggest fan, wife Laura.
(Photo courtesy Carla Jansen.)

being. The story doesn't end there.

Upon graduation J.J. signed with the Green Bay Packers, my favorite team when I was growing up. He was eventually traded to the Carolina Panthers, where he is a solid fixture for them.

J.J. Jansen taught an astounding lesson. He showed that dreams could be achieved by cultivating just one skill. Only one well-developed skill is necessary if it is indeed an unbelievably developed skill.

Chapter 45

STAYING INVOLVED

JOE

"Ours not to reason why, ours but to do and die."
   -Alfred Lord Tennyson

I don't know Joe's last name, but that really doesn't matter. Where Joe is from all you have to do is mention his first name and everyone knows who you are talking about. In that sense he is kind of like Cher, Madonna or Prince. Mention of a first name says it all. Joe lives in Macungie, Pennsylvania in an upstairs condo as a neighbor to my mother Jessica. He is a wonderful, outgoing, helpful man who helps to carry neighbor's groceries, shovel the snow from around their cars and walk their dogs. He is the helpful guy we should all have in our lives and his neighbors love him and appreciate him.

I met Joe a couple of years ago when I went to visit my mother. The stories of Joe preceded him and I was hoping to meet him. Then it happened. Joe came walking down the sidewalk and we were introduced.

"Tim this is Joe that I told you about. Not only is he a great neighbor but I have to tell you he still works and believe it or not he is ninety-six," she said.

The next thing I saw was Joe tapping my mother on the shoulder replying, "thank you sweetie but I am actually ninety eight".

It was later that day that I saw ninety eight year old Joe (who is now one hundred-one) sitting out waiting for his ride to go to work.

Ninety eight. Strong. Vibrant. Courteous. Personable. Helpful. Involved. I knew the lesson of Joe was put in my life for a reason and what a great lesson it is.

Chapter 46

▲

REAL MEN
DR CHARLES GATTI

"In things pertaining to enthusiasm, no man who is sane who does not know how to be insane on proper occasions".

-Henry Ward Beecher

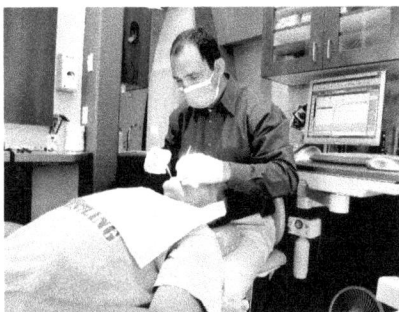

I first met Dr Charles Gatti ten years ago. He is a dentist in Glendale, Arizona. Dr. Gatti is brilliant, hard working, talented and caring. He is a stand-out in his field. That is why I selected him as my dentist, and why I drive over an hour to his office just to get my teeth cleaned. Each time I drive all the way up there I swear it will be my last because it is so far. Each time I leave I know I will be back there because the quality of care and dentistry is so high. There is no way I could ever leave there. I love his professionalism and his ability.

There is something else about him I absolutely love and admire. He is a knucklehead. Please understand this is not a derogatory term. It is a very affectionate one. I am a knucklehead myself. I think the difference is, as boisterous and fired up as I usually am at leading others, people quickly realize I am a knucklehead. It is different with Chuck Gatti. You would never expect it if you knew him only in a professional environment.

So what do I mean by knucklehead? You name it, he'll fight it. If you wanted to fight judo, he would fight judo and he competed at such. If you wanted to do Brazilian ju-jitsu, he would fight that style. In fact, some nights he rides his bicycle to the MMA lab, for the kickboxing class, followed by a beginning Brazillian ju-jutsu class and the advanced BJJ class, all before his bicycle ride home. If you want to fight mixed martial arts, he'll oblige you there. It simply does not matter what the style or rules are or how brutal it gets. Further, it doesn't matter if the experience levels are significantly different. If you are very well trained at something for many years and he is not, he steps up to the challenge anyway. To top it all off, in his 40s he fought some pretty brutal full contact kick boxing matches under the fight name, "The Extractor".

I love Dr. Charles Gatti. To me he symbolizes what we all should be professionally. I also love "The Extractor". To me the knucklehead side represents a fulfillment in living life we should all emulate. In my eyes he is a real man, alive and full of life, working professionally and performing personal challenges to the highest level. In my eyes, real men conquer whatever is set out in front of them. How can you not love a real man like Dr. Chuck Gatti, "The Extractor"?

Chapter 47

DECEPTION

ANTWAAN RANDLE-EL

"All warfare is based on deception."
   -Sun Tzu, *The Art of War*

I have been blessed to not only meet, but also to coach (for short periods of time), Antwaan Randle-El. Football fans will be familiar with Antwaan. He was a standout quarterback at Indiana University, drafted for his athleticism. For non-sports fans, this means he was thought to be too small to be a successful quarterback in the NFL, but was so talented as an overall athlete that owners, coaches, and scouts alike thought he could be converted to other positions, and he'd still be more successful than most of those who have played their positions throughout their entire high school and college careers. This was the case with "El." He was drafted by the Pittsburgh Steelers and successfully converted to a wide receiver.

I worked with El in two-week spurts over two summers. Although a Pittsburgh Steeler, he came to Phoenix with Donovan McNabb, an All-Pro quarterback with the Philadelphia Eagles at the time, to tune-up before entering training camp. He struck me as friendly and courteous, generally happy. This chapter is not about his off-field traits, though. This chapter is about his abilities on the field, specifically the success he has attained via deception. As Sun Tzu wrote in 2650 BC in *The Art of War*, "All warfare is based on deception." This describes Randle-El's gift and the reason he became a huge success in the NFL with a less than ideal height and weight. El developed the uncanny ability to trick even the most efficient tacklers to move in precisely the direction he wanted at precisely the moment he decided to go the opposite direction. His method of achievement was his feet.

At about 10:30 in the morning on a hot summer day in Phoenix, I had players engaged in a competition-based drill in which one player had to run a football across the goal line without letting his opponent touch him, as if in a game of tag. I was in charge of pairing the players to compete against each other and could pair them up as I saw fit. This included me setting up interesting matches, such as a matchmaker in boxing would do. With a huge number of professional players there I knew I could make this interesting. To me, this was like fantasy camp for strength and conditioning coaches, and I got to see the best in the world demonstrate the very skills that made them stand apart from others. The year before, we all marveled at how El changed directions so fast he seemed to be the only one on the planet who could figure out what he did. Hoping to catch a glimpse of this again the second year, I paired El up with a good collegiate athlete, a linebacker named Sammy Sprague. Sammy came from Phoenix and was one of those hard-nosed athletic guys who would give you every ounce of energy he had. I structured the drill to put the defender in a superior position; El would have to be a magician to get past the goal line.

That particular day I probably put the cones marking width of the goal line a little too close together. Star after star, including Donovan McNabb, Brian Westbrook, and other masters at changing direction, failed to score on their defenders. El alone managed the drill. Despite the drill being stacked in the defender's favor, El scored so quickly as to leave Sammy Sprague confused and the rest of us with mouths wide open. Nor did he fail to amaze us with his second rep. Not one of us could articulate exactly what he did, but Sammy didn't manage to tag him.

With so many competitive athletes around so close to the start of the season, the suspense grew as the third rep approached. El had Sammy so confused that this otherwise outstanding athlete fell right on his face; El had scored again. Those of us who saw the drill looked at each other as if to say, what exactly did he just do? Poor Sam stood up with his head downward as if he had just become worthless."Hey, keep your head up," Donovan McNabb said, ever considerate. "He does that to the whole NFL." In that moment I had seen best from both players. Donovan, ever Donovan, could take a man at his lowest moment and put things back into perspective, restoring dignity and pride. And El was indeed a magician, practicing the deception that enabled him to play in the NFL, return punts for touchdowns, and become the only wide receiver to throw a touchdown pass in Super Bowl history. His success at warfare was indeed based on deception, as Sun Tzu had suggested.

Chapter 48

PERPETUAL GROWTH

FRED MOORE

"An investment in knowledge always pays the best interest."
   -Benjamin Franklin

There isn't much left in the world of track and field for Fred Moore to accomplish. As an elite-level coach for over five decades, he's seen it all and done it all. He headed the United States Track and Field Coaches Association for years, was the National Junior College Athletic Association Cross Country Coach of the Year, and coach of the National Championship team. He was the head women's coach for a USA vs. Soviet Union dual meet and the head women's coach of the Olympic Sports Festival team. He coached more than forty All-Americans; eight Open National Champions; the 400 meter world record holder; and the winners of the Boston, Chicago, and Tokyo marathons. Anyone who knows track and field knows, or at least knows of, Fred Moore.

I have been fortunate enough to have Fred Moore as a friend and mentor. Every so often I meet him for lunch, and for the price of a good meal, get an hour and a half to pick his brain. He graciously shares his five decades of experience with me, and I hope to model his lifetime of devotion. He tells me stories of the training programs of elite runners like Jim Ryun. He contrasts those programs with the ones used by world-class Kenyans. He tells me how he has changed his running prescriptions over his 50 year coaching career, what works, what he thought would work but yielded little benefits.

Something I find inspiring about Fred is that he always seems just as interested in picking my brain. I have also coached for decades, often with skilled athletes, but I am most certainly not a coach in my 70s with a full lifetime of experience behind me. I am the one honored to be in the presence of a great, successful coach like Fred More. Yet he asks endless questions of me. I conclude from this that Fred never wants to stop being a student of the game. He shows passion for his own betterment as well as the betterment of those he coaches. His passion has led him to become one of the foremost role models in the coaching industry. I share his passion and hope to follow his example as I continue into my next decade of teaching.

▲

Chapter 49

LIFETIME DEVOTION

KENNY WELDON

"The grand essentials of happiness are: something to do, something to love and something to hope for."
    -Allan K. Chalmers

Most any boxing fan recognizes Kenny Weldon's name. He coaches champions. He coached fighters to more World and National Championships than a person can count on fingers and toes combined. I had the pleasure of working with Kenny Weldon for three years when I trained Siarhei Liakovich. When I think of Kenny, the first thing that comes to mind is not the number of champions he has coached, though. Rather, I think of a conversation we had one night at Siarhei's house.

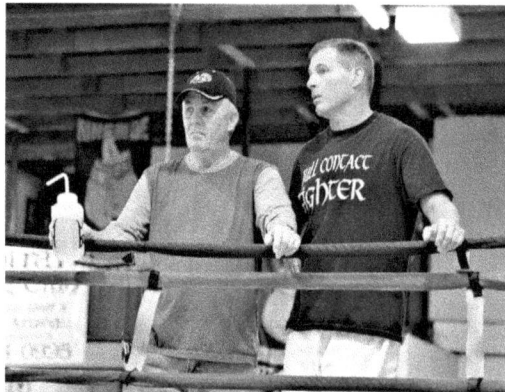

Nine weeks before a big fight, Siarhei was training and he and Kenny decided to watch tapes of previous fights with his opponent-to-be. This struck me as a great educational opportunity for a lot of reasons. I wanted a better understanding of how Siarhei would have to fight so I could prepare his training programs. I also love to pick the brains of older coaches, since they have so much more experience. Beyond that, I thought it would be fun sit around with a world-ranked boxer and coach of World Champions and watch boxing, especially since I am a fighter myself and love any combative activity.

Kenny coaching Siarhei Liakhovich.

We watched the first round of Siarhei's next fighting opponent fighting a different opponent two years earlier. At the end of the first round, Kenny said, "Put the tape in of the next fight," and Siarhei did so. At the end of the first round on that tape, he asked to see the third fight. Two rounds into that tape, Kenny said, "I'll go back and watch all of these tapes with you, but I already know what I need to know."

"How is that?" I asked.

"Tim, I've been in boxing for fifty-five years. Most guys who are in boxing and claim they've been in boxing for thirty or forty years and had a fifteen or twenty year break somewhere along the line. My Daddy brought me up on boxing. I've been in boxing for fifty-five consecutive years. I've had no breaks. I understand fighters."

Fifty-five years. How many people in their lifetime do something consecutively for fifty-five years? I think of all the changes I've made in my life, and I haven't been alive for fifty-five years. Meanwhile, Kenny Weldon has devoted his entire being to boxing longer than I've been alive.

When a human has the sort of passion that consumes, and is willing to commit in the way others are not, they can move mountains. I saw Kenny Weldon take no-name fighter Siarhei Liakovich, who was coming off a loss, and help him become the WBO Heavyweight Champion of the World. Siarhei was blessed to have benefited from Kenny Weldon's lifetime of devotion. I have been blessed as well, to be able to watch.

In the ring, right after Siarhei won the Heavyweight World Championship.

▲

Chapter 50

THE LESSON OF KEEP CLIMBING
LOVIE SMITH

"The will to persevere is often the difference between failure and success."
   -David Sarnoff

Lovie with wife MaryAnne during his tenure at Arizona State.

I remember when Lovie Smith was hired as a new assistant football coach at Arizona State University in 1988. It was always fun to meet new coaches that were hired. Coaching is such a transient profession, it is said by those within the industry that there are two types of coaches: those that get fired and those that are about to be fired. It is more of an industry norm, rather than an exception, for a coach to have to move ten times over a 30-year span.

When I first met Lovie he impressed me as a kind, charming, down-to-earth type of guy. I thought he would be a good hire for the staff. At that time the football staff had some brilliant football minds and those were the guys that were going to directly determine the battle plan of the X's and O's. This staff didn't need an ego-driven strategist trying to establish himself as the alpha male, which can sometimes be the case in this aggressive profession. This staff needed a diligent worker who knew his role and was willing to contribute where needed. Lovie Smith was just that man. He was bright, hardworking and, as a coach who really cared about his players, was willing to do whatever he needed to do within his role to make the program succeed. It was not the highest profile role, but Lovie performed it to the best of his abilities. Throughout his years as a coach, he had also coached at Tulsa University, University of Kentucky, University of Wisconsin, Ohio State University and the University of Tennessee. It was a lot of shuffling for a man with a minor role.

As "the cream rises to the top," so did Lovie Smith. He was hired to coach in the NFL as a position coach in Tampa Bay and St. Louis. Deservedly so, his excellence in lesser roles for twenty years and willingness to move at least nine times throughout his career had led him to a position to accept a major role, as head coach of the Chicago Bears in the National Football League. I was especially thrilled to see the Chicago Bears play in Super Bowl in 2007, under the guidance of head coach Lovie Smith. Having first met Lovie in the infancy of his career, I knew he emerged to be the head coach in the Super Bowl from some tough and trying times as an entry level assistant in a losing Arizona State program.

There's a lesson to be learned from Lovie Smith, one in which an entry level guy can become an NFL Coach of the Year, the very pinnacle of his chosen profession worldwide. He serves as a role model for men and women in less renowned positions, reminding them of just how important their roles are and what they can achieve from doing them well. To all those folks, just keep climbing, as Lovie Smith did.

Chapter 51

THE GUY WHO DIDN'T CRY WOLF

MARIO BENNET

"Facts are facts and will not disappear."
-Jawaharial Nehru

I truly enjoyed coaching Mario Bennet, a star player for the ASU basketball team. Though my assistant, Rich Wenner, was responsible for the off-court conditioning of the men's basketball team, I had a good amount of contact with Mario over the years.

Mario worked hard and did everything we asked of him. He also had an easygoing side that blurred the typically strict coach-to-athlete relationship. Coaches enforce that relationship because athletes who are too comfortable sometimes stop responding to commands. Mario never let our friendship affect his work ethic.

Mario came in to visit me one day and sat in the guest chair of my office. Rich heard Mario's voice and joined us. I knew I was in for fun because Mario and Rich were both enjoyable to be around, more so when they were together.

"Coach, I'm having a serious problem," Mario said. Rich and I looked at each other as if to ask, what is he cooking up now? Is he messing with us again, or serious?

"What's wrong, Mario?" Rich asked.

"They just won't pass me the ball." Here we go again, I thought. Another basketball player complaining that he doesn't get to shoot the ball enough. I am no basketball coach, and I don't proclaim to be, but I do know that every player on the team wants more shots than they actually get. Here goes poor Mario, I thought, into the, "I'm great. Pity poor me because I don't get to shoot the ball enough" pitch. I wasn't in the mood for the pity-the-star-athlete routine. I've heard it way to many times.

"Mario, you are out of your mind," I said. "You are having a great season."

"Coach, I can score on most of these guys when I want to and I could be doing so much better. I swear to you the guards just won't pass me the ball," he said.

This only intensified my disinterest in pitying Mario, so I went for a line I thought would end the conversation faster. "Well, why doesn't Coach Frieder tell these guys to pass you the ball more and put an end to it?"

"He does. He does. He tells them to pass the ball to me more, but they won't do it," he said.

The conversation continued for another thirty minutes. Rich echoed his feelings and I grew more cynical as Mario grew more steadfast in his assertions. When Mario left, Rich and I were both relieved. We loved Mario, but had just finished a seventy-hour work week and didn't have time or energy to deal with such absurdity. Why on earth wouldn't the two guards, Stephen "Headache" Smith and Isaac Burton, want to pass the ball to Mario, who was certainly the team's top scorer and offensive threat? How could they put their team in a position to win otherwise? The story was too unbelievable, and Rich and I were not buying what Mario was selling.

A year later, after federal investigations, Rich and I sat down to eat our words. Mario Bennet was right. They really weren't passing him the ball. It turns out Headache had acquired quite the gambling debt and had been convinced by a bookie that he could erase the debt if he could make ASU lose games. He and Isaac were in the deal together, and were in the perfect position to control the game and miss lots of shots, putting other teams in a better position to win.

This came to a head in a game against the University of Washington in which ASU was down by a significant margin by half time. Federal agents found a staggering amount of money bet on the University of Washington by college kids from Tempe. Usually somewhat meaningless games (in terms of the championship picture) aren't heavily bet on. When the coach and team were notified of the investigation at half time, the guilty players turned the game around and blew out the University of Washington.

Headache and Isaac were nice kids at the time. I enjoyed working with both of them and never would have expected criminal activity from either. Equally surprising was that they really were keeping the ball from Mario, and that Mario had no idea what was going on. Had we actually listened to Mario, thought about it deeply, perhaps we could have figured out what was actually going on. Instead, we dismissed him as one more athlete wanting the limelight and glory. We never expected that Mario really wasn't crying wolf. I'll think twice from here on out.

▲

Chapter 52

PERSISTENCE

SUPER PAIGE

"To climb steep hills requires slow pace at first."
  -William Shakespeare

Several years back, a woman named Dee Dee Mittlestaedt called me and asked about bringing in her daughter, Paige, a junior high school athlete. She arrived a few hours later with a tall, lanky young girl with ribbons in her hair that indicated to me that she played volleyball.

The kid was six feet tall and was just shy of her thirteenth birthday. I thought, ten to one, she would be one of those typical tall and skinny kids who grew so fast that she would lack the muscular strength to propel her mass and the coordination to do so with great accuracy. On top of that, Paige seemed so sweet in demeanor I wondered if she would get through the rigors of the program. I had something of a battle going on inside my head because I liked the mother and daughter so much, but common sense told me that it would be a long shot for Paige to be ultra successful.

Once we started the workout, my suspicions were confirmed. She had only an average amount of natural athleticism. Moreover, I learned that the junior high school team she played on, St. Francis Xavier, was only an average team and though Paige was six feet tall, she was not the team's star. A five foot six inch girl was their MVP.

Paige and I got to work, often with her cousin Amy and a few other volleyball players her own age. I had just finished my career coaching an intense collegiate strength program, and still coached in a pretty fired-up manner. Looking back, I realize now that these girls weren't ready for me and I wasn't ready for them. Regardless, we chipped away at the proverbial stone. Three times a week, without fail, Dee Dee brought her daughter to me and would sit and read for an hour and a half while Paige and I worked and tried to figure each other out. This was no easy deal for either of us. I had not yet been exposed to many super sweet, thirteen year old wannabe athletes, and she didn't have a clue which planet I came from.

Still, we chipped at that stone. Paige Mittlestaedt never missed a workout. Before long she was training two hours per session, three days per week. She started making huge gains. Paige then elected to go to Xavier College Preparatory, Arizona's powerhouse, and she made the varsity volleyball team as a freshman. A month after that, she was named a starter. The following year she started again and during her club ball season she was asked to play two levels higher than her chronological peers. Her junior year she made First Team All-State honors and received hundreds of letters from interested colleges all over the country. Her senior year, she was a wrecking machine. Good hitters have a kill percentage of about thirty percent. Paige's was just under sixty percent. Now at 6'3" and 165 pounds she possessed the build of an elite college player. She played her whole senior season like a college player among high school girls. It almost didn't seem fair at times, but it sure was fun for us.

Did we get lucky, that this once shy, skinny girl grew into a 6'3" woman? Yes. She would have ended up 6'3" whether or not she ever lifted a weight, did speed and agility drills or did plyometric drills until she got light-headed.

Paige's success was not all in her height though. Paige's success can be attributed primarily to her persistence. At the age of thirteen, Paige trained an hour and a half to two hours, three times a week, with someone she thought came from another planet, in addition to extensive volleyball practices. At fourteen, she trained harder yet, again, never missing a workout, even when she had severe injuries, like ankle sprains. She simply refused to miss her workouts, no matter how hard they were or how fired up I was. When she turned fifteen, we increased the intensity, as we did when she turned sixteen, seventeen and eighteen. Persistent Paige kept chipping away. Some of her friends, who had started with her at age thirteen, had quit training and quit volleyball altogether. Others had started at sixteen and trained hard, but didn't train for enough years to make the accomplishments Paige made. Only Paige started early, trained hard, never missed and trained all the way through high school graduation. Only Paige was the two-time All-State winner and received offers from hundreds of colleges to play college volleyball. Only Paige earned the full athletic scholarship to a PAC-10 school (ASU).

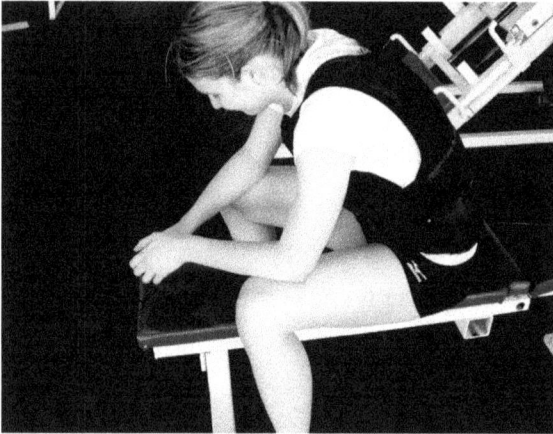

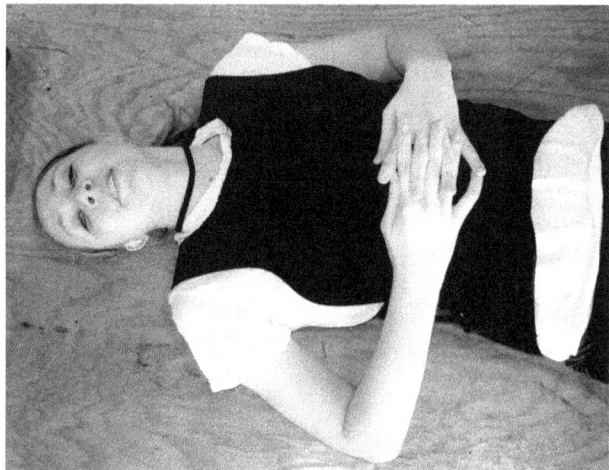

Due to her work ethic Paige finished her high school senior year lifting some seriously heavy weights. When challenged by a star male basketball player from Brophy College Preparatory, Paige not only lifted the same weights he did (seventy pounds in the dumbbell French press, dumbbell pullover and bent over dumbbell row), she completed double the repetitions (the basketball player got four reps each, Paige did eight). Paige took this strength onto the court and played exceptional volleyball. To many in the area, she was known as "Super Paige." Super Paige, your accomplishments were above and beyond others because your persistence was above and beyond others. Thank you for providing a lesson to a man you thought was from another planet.

▲

Chapter 53

WELLNESS

NORM DOMINGUEZ

"Don't just live the length of your life. Live the width of it as well."
　-Diane Ackerman

I met Norm Dominguez under bizarre circumstances. I was in the midst of running an intense workout with twenty or so collegiate and high school athletes. The quality of work that day would make the most disciplined strength coach proud. Every athlete was drenched in sweat and the atmosphere seemed electric. I wake up for these days, when I can help kids access that discipline and power that makes them better athletes and human beings.

I heard rumbling at the front door and in walked a man with a long ponytail and huge smile. His smile was so big I figured he had to be either way too happy or just goofy. Regardless, I didn't want to be interrupted.

"Hi, you must be Tim," he said. "I'm Norman." He knew my name and apparently came in specifically for me. I was trapped.

I tried to figure him out. He looked too old to be interested in the program.

He didn't dress as a professional so I ruled out him being in a peer group. I didn't see anything in his hands to indicate soliciting. I wondered what he wanted. Turns out, Norm was a thirty-eight year old college senior wanting to do an internship under my guidance. He didn't look overly muscular, which made me think he might not have the required weight training experience. He hadn't called to set up an appointment. Finally, I believe in the old adage, "Don't dress for the job you have. Dress for the job you want." Norman hadn't dressed up in the least. I asked him what career path he expected to find himself on and he said, "wellness," to me. My program was not really orchestrated to provide health and wellness. It was strictly for high performance, as in, we are going to out perform you.

My intuition told me to pass on bringing Norm on board, as it requires a great number of hours for me to educate interns, and this just didn't feel right.

Still, first impressions can be tricky, so I made the decision to interview him a week later. I'm glad I did. I found that Norm has a sincere passion for life and everything he does. He loves every minute of every day as if he is trying to squeeze each last drop out of it. I found this to be endearing and thought he might just end up making a good leader of others. Needless to say, I agreed to mentor him during the time of the internship.

Norm's story is this: when he graduated from high school, Norm spent ten years as an amateur boxer, with huge success. His amateur win percentage was over 90% in approximately fifty fights. He was a hopeful for the Olympic Trials and often woke up as early as three-thirty in the morning to get in his daily roadwork.

During that time, he learned about the corruption endemic to certain pockets of boxing. He met those who had taken too many punches to the head and had lost mental functioning to various degrees. He also spent time in ratty gyms, among those who had neither great education nor happiness. He saw the drug use and alcoholism. He saw a lot of unhealthy people in boxing. He also saw a lot of unhealthy people in the construction field, which he was doing for a living at that time. He saw the apathy, dishonesty and downright cheating that goes on within that field. He was essentially surrounded by a high number of unhappy people doing bad things. He wanted no part of it. He desired only health, happiness and success. He had indeed learned about wellness in the sweaty boxing gyms and ditches he was digging in, but it was learning from a reverse angle. He knew what he didn't want. He saw it daily.

It was at this time he met Alicia Maher, who became his sweetheart and eventually his wife. Alicia wanted Norm to have his wellness and to help others with theirs so they decided he should go back to college and get a degree in the field. He did just that.

Norman Dominguez endured ten years of broken noses, a torn rotator cuff and a beaten body. He spent time in the company of those who had suffered much head trauma in boxing. He also spent a decade digging ditches, laying bricks and fighting to get payment for his labor in the construction field. Somehow those difficult times shaped him into the wonderful, mellow, sincere and caring person who thinks first of the health and wellness of others. It's a bigger picture. It is through his example I have stopped focusing exclusively on performance opt-

imization for myself and for others, and have devoted more time towards human wellness. It's the same thing we all need to do better at--focusing on the wellness (mental and physical) of others, as well as our own.

This world needs a lot more guys like Norm Dominguez. It would be a much happier, relaxed and healthy place. I would have never guessed this guy would become one of my most cherished friends and teachers the day he walked in with that big smile.

Chapter 54

ABOVE AND BEYOND THE NORM

MATT MILLEN

"Give me one firm spot on which to stand and I will move the earth."
-Archimedes

Not a day goes by that I don't get to work with a phenomenal professional athlete. But my childhood was nothing like that. I grew up in Guthsville, Pennsylvania, and I never so much as saw a professional athlete, let alone talk to or train with one, as some of the adolescents in my programs do. Just knowing that a major college or professional athlete came from our area was a big deal.

The biggest name in the area then was Matt Millen, a linebacker from Whitehall, Pennsylvania, who went on to start as a linebacker for the Penn State University football team. Every kid in Lehigh Valley knew of this miraculous feat, that someone from Lehigh Valley made it far enough to play at Penn State. As fate would have it, my brother attended Penn State University and lived in dorm a few doors down from Matt Millen. They became friends, and at some point, Matt told my brother, Keith, that he owned Keith a favor. Keith knew exactly how Matt could repay him.

He asked Matt to take me, his little brother, and an aspiring high school football player, into the gym for a weight lifting workout. Keith couldn't have arranged a better gift.

I had just turned sixteen and I made the three and a half hour drive to State College, Pennsylvania. I spent Friday with my brother and we watched the annual spring football game on Saturday. Matt was dominating in that game, as he always was. Later he would earn a reputation for being the guy who could always win. He would win three Super Bowls on three different teams, the only person in the history of the NFL to do so.

After the game, I had the chance to meet Matt. He came to my brother's dorm in the early evening, and I remember the condition of his body more than anything. His fingers were cut, beat up, twisted and mangled. He had bruises everywhere. Mid-evening approached and though I was thrilled to meet him, it occurred to me that I would never get to lift weights with him. After all he was in an intense spring game and he was very beat up, beat up to the point where nine of his ten fingers were either crooked, broken or badly swollen.

As Matt was leaving that evening, I felt a wave of depression over not getting what had been promised, a chance to lift weights with him. He headed out the door, but quickly came back and said, "I'll be back at ten. We'll go lift weights." I found this hard to believe because I suspected the gym at that time would be closed.

True to his word, Matt Millen showed up. He took me to a huge building called Rec Hall, which was indeed closed -- until Matt ripped the back door open with a powerful thrust. I couldn't believe my eyes; this guy, a legend from our area, just ripped open the back door of a massive building so the two of us could lift weights. He was still beat up from the game he had played earlier that day. By then, I was old enough to know that most other athletes would be out partying that evening, but not Matt Millen. That contributed to his greatness.

Lifting weights alone in the huge weight room with Matt Millen was a sixteen-year-old aspiring football player's dream come true. I spotted him and helped him with his fourth rep at 405 pounds on the bench press at about midnight. In the early hours of the next morning he even did some neck strengthening exercises by having me sit on a chair that sat on his head. I had never seen such a radical training method. I could not have loved it more.

I have never seen Matt again, though I have coached several players who played for him, when he was the Detroit Lions' general manager. Matt Millen had the desire to be great, and the fortitude to be ultra-successful at Penn State. He followed up with an outstanding professional career. When his career ended, he was the only person in the history of the game to have won Super Bowl rings on three different teams that he captained. I learned that this future was not only possible, but probable, that late Saturday night that we broke into Rec Hall. It was all about the effort. I hope all of the young athletes who read this will put that into their hearts as I have.

Chapter 55

COURTESY

SENSEI KASUGA

"Nothing is ever lost by courtesy. It is the cheapest of the pleasures; costs nothing and conveys much. It pleases him who gives and him who receives, and thus, like mercy, it is twice blessed."
  -Erastus Wiman

Sensei Kasuga in blue gi.

I heard stories about Sensei Shun Kasuga for months before I met him, the sort of stories that sound like urban myths: the mysterious, quiet and humble man from Japan tossing around all the big, bad, well-built animals that America had to offer. When I talk about big, bad men, I'm talking about former heavyweight Ultimate Fighting Champion Rico Rodriquez, National Judo Champions Christophe Leininger, Brian Leininger, Eric Udell and Jim Dunning, among others. I'm talking the real deal.

Since stories of old Japanese martial arts masters are so frequently distorted, I thought the stories might be a bit exaggerated as well. We've all heard a lot of these stories and definitely seen plenty of them on video. To the untrained eye, it may seem that a master is throwing at will men half his age, twice his size, twice his weight and twice his strength. In reality, for a lesser rank to not willingly take a fall for an esteemed master would be a horrible breach in etiquette. Knowing this, I prefer to trust my trained eyes. Still, the Shun Kasuga stories intrigued me, because the sources were reliable and at the Leininger dojo where this went on, people were not obligated to observe strict Japanese etiquette. I was doubtful, but a bit curious.

When I arrived to train, I saw that Sensei Kasuga was in his early forties and of average size, maybe 5'8" and 185 pounds. He looked remotely fit, but not astonishingly strong. This particular night was a fighting night, and there was no better place to fight than the Leininger dojo. The Japanese have a saying that fit the philosophy of the Leininger dojo, "jigoku kego." The phrase, roughly translated, means "hell training." At any given night, twenty strong, talented, and somewhat mean black belts occupied the mat in full testosterone rage. This night was no different, and I think others, like me, came to take a crack at Sensei Kasuga.

I fought him first that night and I got tossed. I got up and got tossed again. I got up a third time. I got tossed a third time. So did my Sensei, Christophe Leininger. So did Christophe's brother, Brian, a National Champion in the heavyweight division. So did all the others. At least then I knew the stories were true.

I learned then that a good Japanese judo player can indeed put an opponent into a high amplitude throw without the opponent ever realizing what was happening. While this is indeed a lesson, it is not the lesson I will focus on in this chapter. I found out that Sensei Kasuga had twice coached on the Olympic Games, and I could tell he had spent his entire life doing judo. He had superior technique, but all of that paled in comparison to the courtesy he gave us. He treated each student as if they were the most special student. His patience with the white belts made a particular impression on me; teaching those who just cannot make their bodies do what is asked of them can frustrate endlessly. He treated the intermediate, colored-belt ranks with the courtesy that might be afforded an Olympic champion. As for the black belts, well, we all lined up to attempt to kick his butt. He never treated us that way. When he threw someone in demonstration, he would politely ask that person "would you mind taking a fall?" He would also ask, "May I have the privilege of playing judo with you?" over and over, even while we had our nostrils flared in anticipation of battle. He never used words like "fighting against him," "hell training," or things of that nature. He simply requested the pleasure of playing judo with us.

Unfortunately for us, Sensei Kasuga moved back to Japan to teach and coach judo at a major college. I often marvel at the incongruity; a man capable of taking another man's life always humbly asked to play judo. Certainly most Americans don't approach their competitive ventures that way. I wish everyone playing a sport could access Sensei Kasuga's courtesy lesson. Sensei Kasuga, you have the ability to throw a man, choke him unconscious, and presumably, take a life. But you also have an even more amazing ability to show courtesy, represent man as he should be and to give life. Thank you for being a great role model. May you find everything your heart desires in Japan.

Chapter 56

CROSSING CULTURAL BARRIERS

SIMEON EKRISSON

"We must live together as brothers or perish together as fools."
    -Martin Luther King

Simeon and I sharing our award at the Grand Canyon State Games. Sensei Ted Rabino (on left) presented teh award.

A surprise waited for me at the 2007 Grand Canyon State Games karate tournament, which are the most highly attended state games in America. The surprise came in the form of an award, an award given to athletes with extraordinary character. Quite honestly, my karate is not award-worthy, but I was honored to have been selected from a pool of so many great practitioners for this. My co-recipient was none other than my teammate, Simeon Ekrisson. This gave the award more meaning; Simeon has been a great friend and teammate for many years, and we often trained together, a mutually beneficial arrangement.

It occurred to me that the odds must be slim of two guys who are so completely different sharing the same award. Simeon grew up in Africa, his birthplace; I was born in Pennsylvania. Simeon is black; I am white. Simeon is fast; I am slow. Simeon speaks many languages; I sometimes struggle with English. Simeon's karate is physical; my karate is mental. Simeon is quiet; I am loud. Simeon does only karate; I do many arts. Yet, in many ways we function as brothers.

Simeon and I have actually shared many accomplishments together. Often he would win the fighting portion of the men's open black belt division and I would win the fighting portion among black belts over forty. As teammates, along with Kyle Harder and Jihone Du, we often won the black belt team division. Still, my fondest memory of him doesn't come from accomplishments, but rather from the 25th Annual Wado-Ryu Sportsmanship Invitational Tournament.

For the first and only time in karate, judo, jujitsu or sombo, my wife, Janet, and I fought in the same tournament. Fight time approached, and as usual, I was not in the mood to talk to anybody and, yes, that included my wife. I had been on a roll winning matches all year and I expected a lot of myself. Besides that, Kelly Chipman was fighting in my division, and he has better skills than I do. Needless to say, I was in a different mental zone when it came time for Janet to fight. I was focused on my performance, not hers. Simeon, being Simeon, jumped in to coach her. He had high spirits and catchy enthusiasm, and his technical advice was dead on. Janet upset a couple of more experienced fighters that day and won the woman's brown belt championship. Simeon did an amazing job that day---my job. I really should have been coaching her, not only as a "superior" in karate, but also as her husband. When I was off, too focused on my own challenges, Simeon (who also was competing and had his own challenges upcoming) did the forthright thing I had failed to do in helping my very own wife. To those who knew all of us, it may have seemed absurd to see Tim punching the wall to warm himself up while some guy, originally from

another continent, coached Tim's wife. In fact, reflecting back upon it, it even seems a little odd to me. But, that was Simeon being Simeon, a dear friend looking after the wife of his teammate.

I have a great deal of respect for Simeon Ekrisson. He left his home, family, and friends to make a better living in America, but not for himself. He takes the money he makes and sends it back to Africa to give his friends and family a better life. In doing so he has touched many others as well.

Thank you, Simeon, for becoming a citizen of the United States. You have enhanced our dojo, our city and our lives. You crossed cultural barriers, braved the tough times you started out with in America and have helped dozens of people in the process. One of these is me, and I will do a better job of reaching out to others in the future, as a result of your lesson.

▲

Chapter 57

REUNITING

THOMASINE FALCONE

"We must all hang together or assuredly we will all hang separately."
-Benjamin Franklin

In the late 1970s and early 1980s, I sometimes attended classes at East Stroudsburg State College with another physical education major, Thomasine Wargo. I did not know Thomasine well. We never really interacted socially and had more of an acquaintance-ship than a friendship. En route to getting our degrees, we took three or four classes together, and so we sometimes talked about classes but that was pretty much it.

When I graduated I moved to Arizona from Allentown, Pennsylvania to pursue a career of coaching elite athletes. I didn't know what became of Thomasine. About two decades after college, an article appeared in The Morning Call, my childhood hometown's paper, about how I had trained Donovan McNabb and quite a few other Philadelphia Eagles players. The reporters thought it made a nice human interest story, the "local guy" training the professional athlete that was the hero of the area. The article was well done and it was nice to have a few former friends and acquaintances in the area contact me because of it.

Thomasine happened to read the article and she wrote to me. She still lived in eastern Pennsylvania and she taught physical education in the Pleasant Valley school district. I was surprised that she wrote; I didn't know her that well, but I was also touched that she had taken the time and effort to find my contact information and follow through on correspondence.

Since that time, we have cultivated an email friendship—perhaps the friendship we didn't cultivate in college because we were both too busy. I've gotten to learn about her outstanding teaching career, the vast number of East Stroudsburg University students she has mentored, the many academic and athletic successes of her sons and even that her husband coached for a while with my beloved high school coach Tom Filipovits. One year, while attending a Thanksgiving dinner with my in-laws, I found out that Thomasine lives next door to Janet's cousins. They called her and she came over to visit us. It was a very touching gesture.

We could have never had that friendship if she hadn't been the one to reach out. I suspected back in the early 80s that she was headed for a great future, now I know for sure. I'm proud to see my classmate and ESSC alum do so well and am forever grateful I can share in it. Thomasine just finished her twenty-ninth year as a teacher. She is a great teacher. I know. She sure taught me a lesson.

▲

Chapter 58

CUSTOMER SERVICE

TOM BERGMAN

"He profits most who serves best."
    -Arthur F. Sheldon, motto for Rotary International

Early in my career, customer service seemed irrelevant to me. I was driven to discover the exercises, routines and programs that would work best for the athletes I trained, and to that end, I looked to scientific literature being published about athletics. I wanted knowledge and at the time, I thought that knowledge alone would be enough to make me an outstanding strength and conditioning coach. Tom Bergman taught me that knowledge, while infinitely valuable, is meaningless in a profession like mine if not enthusiastically conveyed and dynamically put into use, a loving use no less. Strangely, this essential link between athletes and coaches is rarely taught in undergraduate or graduate curriculum.

The late Tom Bergman became a friend of mine after I started providing his daughter, Dana, with strength training and conditioning coaching. Fourteen at the time, Dana wanted to be a better high school volleyball player. Dana was in my original group of volleyball girls, the group that started with me when I first started my own business. At the time, I was just out of my college coaching days, and going through a phase that involved some seriously intense protocols.

I met Tom only after a year of training Dana. Owner of a construction company, Caliente Construction, Tom was a self-made man. Enthusiastic and energetic, I think he mentioned in every conversation that if I should ever need anything, I could contact him. He had a genuineness and warmth about him that made an impression on me. Tom never preached to me about customer service, never gave me seminars, clinics, or magical books that could turn me into a customer service machine. But through his actions, he taught me that we should all be customer service machines. Customer service is a means of respecting and honoring others, whether they are your parents, friends, people you don't know or actual customers with whom you do business. Tom taught me this by being Tom, the best of customer service machines.

At some point, Janet and I decided our old roof was showing signs of wear and tear, and we needed to replace it. I called Tom to ask if he had any recommendations, and he said he would come out on Saturday morning between nine and ten to take a look. He promised to find me the best roof for the best price and to draw up intricate bid specifications to ensure high quality. I told Tom he didn't need to inconvenience himself by driving all the way out to my house and take up the few precious hours he had off on Saturday morning. He insisted. He treated me like the most important person on earth, exactly how he always treated me.

That Saturday I was in a large building on the back of my lot, which was matted, and served as our martial art training dojo. I was preparing a couple of fighters for the Ultimate Fighting Championships and several others for state and national competitions in judo and karate. At ten thirty or so I looked up at the clock and realized I had not heard from Tom, and was shocked. Tom always treated me like the king of the universe, yet he was half an hour past his own deadline and nowhere to be found. Honestly, I was a little disappointed. A few minutes later, I got a drink and opened the door to spit out some water, but, when I looked out the door, I spotted Tom on my roof, notepad and measuring tape in hand.

"Tom," I yelled. "Sorry I didn't see you. You should have come back and gotten me. When did you get here?"

"About an hour ago, Tim," he said. "I didn't want to disrupt your training. I know how important that is to you. I brought my own ladder and figured I had work to do, so I just got after it."

This was Tom Bergman. He put others first. He worked hard. He served. In that way, Tom Bergman taught me what customer service should be like. I'm proud to say that soon after Tom Bergman taught me that lesson, I improved my customer service skills. Soon after, his daughter Dana came to me and said, "Don't tell my parents I was here today."

"Why not, Dana? I have to bill them for this session," I said.

"Because I stole my mom's car. I wanted to train so badly and I didn't have a ride otherwise. So I just took it."

Horror was my initial reaction. I did not want to be the cause of this young girl stealing her mother's car. Then I thought about how badly this kid wanted to train. She was willing to go through some pretty great lengths to make it happen. She was my customer, literally, and I was obligated to provide her with the sort of customer service that Tom had taught me to provide. This thing was going full circle. Then something else hit me.

"Congratulations, Dana," I blurt out, with enthusiasm. "I didn't realize you turned sixteen and can now drive."

"I didn't, Tim. I'm still fifteen," she said, something I never expected to hear.

So now I had a fifteen-year-old athlete, driving illegally, in a car she stole from her mother because she wanted to train with me, because I was providing the customer service I had learned from her own father. Fascinating. Oh…I probably should add that the car was a Lexus.

Years later, Tom Bergman lost his battle with cancer. At the memorial service, many people commented that God needed Tom's help, and that is why Tom was called to him. His customer service was simply that good, and so was his example.

▲

Chapter 59

KNOWING YOUR ROLE

TOMMY BROOKS

"Knowledge of our duties is the most essential part of the philosophy of life."
  -George W. Goethals

I often tell my athletes that performance improves when "coaches coach, officials officiate, competitors compete." Too many athletes get caught up worrying about their coaches decisions and the officials calls.

Coaches should coach within their expertise. As a strength and conditioning coach, I feel that a tennis coach, for example, should coach the technical and tactical components of tennis. The tennis coach should then communicate fitness observations to the strength coach. When the tennis coach assumes responsibility for post-play sprints, conditioning, plyometrics and core training -- and then sends the athlete to the strength coach -- the duplicate training can hinder or injure the athlete. Additionally, the over-trained or injured athlete senses the lack of coordination and feels that his or her best interests are not priority to those responsible for optimizing their performance. I've had this done to me too many times and it has never been good.

While at Arizona State University, an arrogant assistant football coach would write supplemental workouts for his position players on a grease board on the weight room wall. He didn't have the best interest of his players at heart; he wanted to be recognized as the ring leader. He would come in Tuesday and write up exercises such as bench press, flies and dips, exercises his players would have done already the previous day. The players recognized that repeating these exercises on Tuesday wouldn't help them progress, and they knew their leader didn't know what he was doing. He ended up looking foolish and losing the trust of those he should have led, as well as alienating me in my role as strength and conditioning coach.

A great leader, on the other hand, surrounds himself with a quality staff. A leader's decision-making process, hiring choices and competent leadership style all contribute to success. Great leaders recognize the talents of others and allow them to tap in to those talents.

Tommy Brooks qualifies as a great leader. Tommy has been involved in boxing most of his life. He's done everything from the fighting itself to wrapping hands and emptying spit buckets to coaching multiple World Champions. I worked with Tommy in 2005 while he coached World Champion Vasilliy Jirov. Tommy and I met several times to prepare his training camp, at which time we defined our roles. Once we did, we got right to work.

I never told Vasilliy how to throw his jab or what tactical approach to use in the ring. Tommy Brooks never said a word during Vassiliy's strength and conditioning workouts. For six weeks, Tommy came into the weight room daily and gave me a rundown of Vassiliy's physical state. Then he pumped me up so Vassiliy would have the best care. When the workout started, Tommy watched for two hours, saying nothing. While Vassiliy and I were in the weight room, I was responsible for providing the expert guidance. There was never interference.

As I reflect on my time with Tommy, I'm reminded of another coach. Greg Hull, as I wrote in *Inner Strength Inner Peace*, taught me the necessity of performing my own role, and only my own role. Tommy knew his role was to provide the technical and tactical components of boxing coaching. He did not think he had all the answers in all fields. His leadership came from creating a team that worked together, from delegating responsibility and from trusting. Having seen this, I understand how he ascended to the top of his profession and I hope to do the same for my athletes.

Chapter 60

"LOVING THOSE YOU SUPERVISE"

DAN HEEFNER

"Do more than you're supposed to do and you can have or be or do anything you want."
   -Bill Sands

Approximately ten years ago I received a phone call from a former professional baseball player that I had helped coach, Eric Newman. Eric had since retired from playing baseball and had become employed as the head baseball coach at Dallas Baptist University. Quite honestly, I had never heard of the school before. But I really liked and believed in Eric, and so when he asked me if I would fly in to consult on their strength and conditioning program, I jumped in right away.

Before I got there Eric gave me a run down of the place and told me his lead assistant at the time was Dan Heefner, a young coach who had a gift for helping others. That is exactly what I found when I met him.

To this day, I'm in contact with DBU Head Coach Heefner several times a year. The phone call always starts out with him saying, "I have a question for you," --clearly implying he wants my help. The conversation always ends with me having tried my best to provide my opinions and insights, but feeling like I got so much more out of the phone call than Dan did.

Simply put, Dan Heefner loves the players he coaches. He loves them so much he is on a never-ending search to find any one item, no matter how small, that can help better them as either players or as people. Coach Heefner has never come to me without full knowledge of a subject area, such as training the rotator cuff, preventing anterior cruciate injuries with exercises, or maximizing bat head speed while batters are swinging at pitches. Rather, he has thoroughly researched all of the areas he asks me about. In fact, I sometimes feel like he knows so much more about them than I do because of his extensive researching. He just can't help himself; he has to do everything he can possibly do in order to better his athletes. Ninety-nine percent effort just isn't good enough for him to give when he is attempting to help those he coaches. He has to continually strive to learn more, to be better because he loves his players so much and he wants them to be their best. He has to ask me, even if he is extremely knowkledgable. It's who Dan Heefner is.

I have often wondered if the folks at Dallas Baptist University know how lucky they are to have Dan Heefner leading its baseball team. I often think of how lucky I am to have him leading me by his example. I hope some day at least one of my athletes feels that I try as hard for them as Dan Heefner does for his entire team.

Dan, by the time you read this, I'll probably not have learned anything new about the rotator cuff, but call me anyway. I always like learning from you.

Chapter 61

HANDLING PHYSICAL AND MENTAL PAIN
DAN LAFOND

"I've never known anybody to achieve anything without overcoming adversity."

   -Lou Holtz

(Photo courtesy CoastPhoto.com)

Dan LaFond is a good friend of mine. He has been for over twenty years. I could not think more highly of him. We first competed as opponents in the karate dojo and in tournaments. We fought long. We fought hard. It was pretty brutal. Actually, it was more than pretty brutal at times, it was super brutal. Dan is about six foot six and two hundred and fifty pounds of muscled up, lean fighting machine with good skills. I always had to be on top of my game with him because of this. Add to this that I get a little more fired up fighting the giants and we've had some clashes that were quite memorable. Despite this, I cherish the guy because he is just an exceptional person and wonderful friend. When he asked me in 2010 to help him train for the Police/Firefighter World Games I jumped at the chance.

It sounds like a fun job, training a fantastic person for a huge international sporting contest, but it wasn't. It was tough. Super tough. It stretched me professionally to provide the right service for this guy.

Dan hadn't done karate for many years…about ten. He had three badly herniated discs and worse yet, the doctor who performed the surgery to fix them actually botched it up. At first, the doctor had an intern doing the work and, after screaming at the intern during the surgery for not doing it as the doctor had wished, the doctor himself decided to finish the rest. We know this for fact. Dan heard all of this himself, despite being under anesthesia. Apparently there are some times when patients under anesthesia cannot talk, but are fully coherent of everything going on. This was one of those. Worse yet, weeks after the surgery, Dan had no relief. He told this to the doctor only to have him say, "The MRI looks fine to me, we're done talking." That doctor then stormed out of the room. Ouch.

So, despite the botched surgery and the decade off, we set out in pursuit of Dan's goal. We got started, this time with a rusty and slower Dan than I used to war with.

To make matters worse, we had problems along the way. Dan broke a toe and missed two weeks of training. We worked diligently to recover, but his back would only permit us to work so long and so hard. The kicker was Dan breaking a second toe in the last hard karate workout just one week before the contest. He literally registered for the contest in a walking boot. It was one he tried to hide under a bell-bottom shaped pair of sweat pants, as if that would solve the problem. Add to that his constant, relentless back pain from the herniated discs and unsuccessful surgery and you have quite a challenge to get through.

Against all odds Dan won a silver medal in the World Games, despite having every reason not to even think about competing. His only loss came to the champion, a remarkable fighter from Norway. What an accomplishment for a guy with three herniated discs, a major surgery that did nothing and two broken toes.

Of course, there is a lesson, a very valuable lesson, to learn from Dan. He had a dream. He worked long and hard for it to come to fruition. Along the way he faced extreme adversity—adversity that would make most quit. He never saw quitting, he only saw overcoming. Not coincidentally, he overcame.

Previously, I said it wasn't easy training him. The word I would now use to describe training him was "rewarding," or "enriching." What a great life lesson from great person...one of the world's best.

▲

Chapter 62

TRUST WORKS

ROSIE

"To be trusted is a greater compliment than to be loved."
    -George MacDonald

If you have read this book's predecessor, *Inner Strength Inner Peace*, you may have come to the conclusion that my wife Janet is a dog collector. This would be accurate. To date we have had six dogs, all Labrador Retrievers, most recent of which is named Rosie (named after the AC/DC song "Whole Lotta Rosie" because she was quite fat as a puppy).

In my previous book, I referred to White Dog as the cutest puppy ever, but Rosie was just as cute. She is now one and a half years old and to this date we frequently hear comments about how she belongs in commercial ads or on television advertisements. Better yet is the fact that she has been so calm, so loyal, so loving. We have marveled that she is always lying

down side by side with one of the other dogs or is lying on our feet, most frequently Janet's since she works from home. We've formed a bond with Rosie that is quite strong.

While she appears so far to be a perfect dog (and is indeed pretty close) I have struggled with her sometimes. The struggles have come when I call her name and sometimes she just hasn't cared to come to me. These disappointments have in turn caused me more than once to comment to Janet, "you really need to train your dog a little better, it seems she doesn't even know her own name." (Yes, she gets called Janet's dog when she misbehaves and my dog when she's angelic.)

It wasn't until she was fourteen months old that we noticed the times she didn't respond to our calls were only when her back was turned to us. Then the proverbial "ah ha" light of genius seem to flash on over our heads. Perhaps she has a partial hearing loss, we thought. We were wrong.

Our beloved little girl is completely deaf in both ears. This was confirmed by a veterinary hearing specialist.

Looking back it all makes sense. She couldn't respond to our calls when our back was turned. She could not hear us and could not see us with her back turned. Since then we have pieced together a greater understanding of how she functions. By placing her trust in us or her fellow canine companions (she is usually touching one of us or Geronimo and Musashi), she senses movement to arouse her from sleep. She is therefore always alerted when she needs to be. Some call these dogs "Velcro dogs" because they are always "stuck

to you". She has learned her commands such as sitting, shaking, lying down, speaking and others from watching our other dogs. Essentially her whole world is built on trust, including her naps. Her trust has served her so well that she is nothing shy of a wonderful, happy, loving, playful and fully functioning pet. None of our friends (including those who come to the house frequently) ever had a clue that this dog was completely deaf. Her mannerisms and demeanor tell us the deafness is of no consequence to her. My writing could never do justice to the puppy playfulness she still exhibits with her "sisters" or to her chucking her rawhide bones all around the back yard in an ecstasy that make us laugh out loud.

Trust. It really works. I wish all those I coached and tried to help could learn from Rosie's example.

Chapter 63

▲

STRENGTH IN UNITY
MY NEW TEAM

"Organizations exist only for one purpose: to help people reach ends together that they couldn't achieve individually."
-Robert H. Waterman

In my first book *Inner Strength Inner Peace*, I wrote a chapter about my 2008 teammates, the five guys that reversed a quarter-century losing streak for the Western Region team of the I.S.K.F. and how their unity produced a national karate championship. Three years later, I was afforded another positive life lesson courtesy of a team, only this time it was much different.

I decided in 2010 that my karate was stagnant. The good ole Japanese style taught in Arizona was now obsolete. The Europeans had changed it drastically. I was doing well competitively in tournaments in my old style, but I sensed my competitive career was winding down at fifty years of age and I knew it would be my last chance to develop new skills. I set four very lofty goals as my heart's desire. There are two major karate organizations in the United States that have a National Championships: the AAU and the USA-NKF. My goal was to be on a gold medal winning team in both championships and to also win as an individual in my age group. It was probably a far-fetched dream for someone changing his style drastically.

The first guy I contacted was an acquaintance I really didn't know very well. His name is Doug Jepperson and he is a Senseï in Park City, Utah. Sensei Jepperson has been in karate for over forty years and has coaching skills I could not find in Arizona. He is a brilliant man, is cognizant of the huge metamorphosis of karate sparring and was willing to share his time and expertise. I called him in the best-case scenario hope that he would share some tidbits of information over the phone to help me. He far exceeded that. He invited me to his dojo in Park City and offered me free lodging at his home. Usually, I never accept those invitations as I hate the thought of imposing on others. This time I jumped on it. This opportunity was too good to pass up. I was there a week later, watching karate

Sensei Jepperson with former UFC Champion Rashad Evans.

DVDs until three A.M. and cherishing every minute of it. It was a huge blessing.

What wasn't a blessing, however, was his mention that the physical profile of an elite-performing karate-ka was one as a "tall, skinny guy". I knew what I had to do: strip my body of any remaining fat and even some of the hard-earned muscle tissue. I also knew I had to access the top sports scientist with regard to nutrition, Tom Incledon.

Tom, a brillant scientist.

Tom had been an associate and a friend for many years. I had referred many of the professional athlete clients I serve to him and had seen amazing results. His program is quite challenging but the results are second to none. If I was truly going to be my best, I had to go through Tom. He has no peers. He didn't disappoint me. His advice was so detailed, so technical, so precise. It was also so hard, with requirements of me completely eliminating about five-dozen foods from my diet for one to six months. I had to take supplements (up to twenty pills) three times a day. I carried food everywhere and could not eat at most restaurants. When it was all said and done, I had made dietary changes that were precisely compatible with my own blood. There was no guesswork with Tom—only futuristic scientific precision. I lost twenty pounds, increased my energy level immensely and quadrupled the amount of time I could train. Imagine how confident I became in my skills when I could train four times as long. How could I not trust him? He has both the mind of Einstein and is a knucklehead who competes in strongman contests. He not only knows it, he lives it. Surely he would understand me. He was going to be a huge edge for me. Tournaments are often won by one or two points:

Tom, the knucklehead.

surely Tom would make that difference.

My next call was to my guru of exercise physiology, Dr. Jeff Messer.

I wanted his elite-level knowledge to govern my conditioning off-mat. Since I was going to fight as a lighter guy, I had to be much more active guy and had to be in better shape than anyone else in the country in my age group. The consummate student, Dr. Messer prescribed the perfect supplementary conditioning protocols, and they were all measured with a heart rate monitor and logged. No one knows the physiology of exercise better than Dr. Messer and it shows in the elite level athletes he coaches. I was fortunate to become one of them. I was leaving no stone unturned.

Now the hard part. In Japanese Karate-do etiquette we are taught that lower-ranking students never critique higher-ranking ones. It is nonnegotiable. This brought a problem. All of my sparring teammates are lower-ranking. I had to convince them to tell me where I was wrong and to own my performance, as

175

I owned theirs. I failed miserably. They all clung to the etiquette and/or didn't want any piece of having to coach me. My first two tournaments of 2011 were a disaster for me. I blew a gasket after the second one in a way people would not expect of me, and I was ruthless. Basically put, I was a jerk for a month to my training partners. More specifically, one training session of three hours, I yelled at Liz for an hour straight for not coaching me better and owning my outcome, then talked with her for another hour and then finally we trained for an hour. It was hard on me. Liz is a great training partner. She is a multiple time

Liz scoring at the 2011 Nationals

black belt national champion and has great skill. She is fast, strong and certainly one of the toughest women on earth, if not the toughest. Yet, she was not coaching me to the level an aspiring national champion athlete needs. I was impossible, but -- it worked. Liz started coaching me more and coaching me well. She was putting into my training the same immense effort she always puts in to her own training. I was

getting information on a weekly basis from my beloved Sensei in Utah, whom I gave 100% trust. Tom's diet and supplement program was working. I was reaping the benefits of Jeff Messer's genius. I talked track coach extraordinaire Greg Hull into helping me with a plyometric program to make me more dynamic in my movement. He too was so gracious in the giving of his time and expertise, and his guidance was like gold. He has coached many

Olympic Champions. I knew I was in good hands. It was all headed in the right direction.

The next blessing was getting my old 2008 teammate Jeff "Freight Train" Dodge to help coach me. Let me tell you—you've never met anyone like this guy. He's 6'2", 230 pounds of bone-breaking predator when he's training and 100% goofball when he's not. This was a challenge to get him into owning my performance because he's usually trying to rip my arm off and beat me to death with it when we're in the dojo and then he's a poster child for Goofballs Anonymous when

Freight Train, the predator.

Only Freight Train can don camouflage fake gloves and a young child's headgear.

he's outside the dojo. Seriously, the guy needs a 24-step program: 12 steps for being too amped up and predatory in the dojo and another 12 for being a knucklehead. The good news? I persisted and finally coaxed this creature into owning my outcome. He was coaching me to win. I was improving greatly because of his feedback.

It was at this time I was training so much Tom Indedon hit me with some seemingly bad news—my testosterone count was about a quarter of what he would like it to be and my antioxidant absorption was low. He suggested more

recovery time. I called Koco Garcia of Proformance Health, my favorite licensed massage therapist in this whole world, and scheduled a standing weekly appointment. All I can say about her and her skill level can be summed up in one word: perfection. I think she views me as an eccentric puzzle that she has to solve. If my quadratus lumborum in my lower back hurts and I don't mention it to her, she finds it anyway. If she has cranked down on me unmercifully, exhaustingly for an hour and fifty-five minutes and we have only five minutes remaining, she'll continue to work through extreme pain for ten more minutes, just to ensure she gets my body where it needs to be. I truly believe she has x-ray capability in her hands. She finds things she just shouldn't be able to find by feel. I can't figure out how she does what she does. On top of that she has this weird, atypical desire to serve to perfection that doesn't exist in many people these days. I can sum her up only as a blessing in my life. Her work, literally, is perfection. It is nothing less.

Thankfully, for my training partners' sakes (make that for the sake of everyone who knows me) my tune-up tournament in Salt Lake City went better—still not to my satisfaction—but I didn't have to yell at poor Liz this time. The year ended with me winning nine straight matches against national-class fighters. The team won both national championships as well. Mission accomplished.

2011 AAU National Team Champions: Jeff Dodge, Fred Erickson, Sensei Jepperson, myself, Sean Greene.

There is a huge moral to the story and it is not at all about what Tim McClellan "accomplished." God gave me my genes, Sensei Jepperson gave me his time, his love and his exceptional guidance. Tom Incledon gave me nutritional help second to none. Dr. Messer gave me state-of-the-art conditioning advice. Greg Hull gave me a program that reflected his forty years of being one of the world's top track coaches. Koco was perfect. My wife Janet gave me unconditional support and help. My training partners-turned-coaches Liz and Freight Train denied their instincts and training to help me. The job they did was tough, but they did it incredibly well. Sean Greene and Pat Misch served as training partners for me.

This is not a story about me. It's a story about a team. It's a story of love, expressed through acting first on behalf of others. They did this for me. It's a story of blessings and how fortunate I was to receive so many of them in the midst of my lofty ambition. It is a story of patience, tolerance, overcoming ourselves. It is a lesson in teamwork, and how a team can accomplish things an individual just cannot.

2011 USA-NKF National Team Champions

This is a story that started with desire (me wanting an outcome) and ends in desire (me eagerly wanting opportunities to serve the team that served me so well).

Thank you, all of you. I love you all and hope you'll call on me soon. The joy I'll have in serving you back will far exceed the joy of winning those titles.

Chapter 64

SETTING THE BAR HIGH

ZEKE JONES

"To be good is noble, but to teach others to be good is nobler."
-Mark Twain

(Photo courtesy zekejones.com).

Zeke Jones has accomplished great successes in the sport of wrestling this entire life. A champion high school wrestler, he earned a full scholarship to Arizona State University. At ASU he won multiple NCAA All-American awards. Upon graduation he won a World Championship and placed second in the Olympic Games. Years later he became the head wrestling coach at the

University of Pennsylvania. Today he is the Head Coach of the U.S. Olympic team. A man who has made outstanding achievements like those should be long-remembered for his accomplishments. I certainly have not forgotten those, as well as the lesson he taught me about setting the bar high. I learned this lesson shortly after he returned to Tempe, Arizona from his successful Olympic Games.

"Zeke, congratulations," I said, offering my sincerest happiness.

"For what," he replied.

"For winning a silver medal. You've now been a World Champion and Olympic Silver Medalist."

His response? "I didn't win a silver medal. I lost a gold medal." He was dead serious. That's just how he saw it. He saw only being the best in the world as his standard.

Super successful. Super high standards. Zeke Jones left no doubt. There is a correlation. May we all set the bar high as per his standards.

Chapter 65

▲

INTEGRITY

ERIC NEWMAN

"Have the courage to say no. Have the courage to face the truth. Do the right thing because it is right. These are the magic keys to living your life with integrity."

-W. Clement Stone

It was the height of an era in professional baseball now referred to as the steroid era. Sluggers that once weighed 170 pounds were now weighing in at 230 pounds and more than doubling their output of home runs.

At that time I was training a very promising minor league pitcher named Eric Newman. Eric was blessed with an overabundance of charisma and is such a nice person that you cannot help but love the guy. He was a hard-throwing, right-handed pitcher at 6 foot 2, 215 pounds. He had pitched exceptionally well in the minor league Double-A system and also in the highest of the minor leagues, the Triple-A. When you play that well in either of those leagues you are an instant away from attaining your lifetime dream of playing Major League Baseball. Like 9,000 others in the minor leagues, Eric Newman had that dream and was so close to it he could taste it. He deserved getting that call up into the major leagues. He worked super hard for it and went well above and beyond what others did to get there.

Eric Newman knew about the rampant use of steroids in baseball and he had personally seen many times over that using steroids did indeed make a player a much better player. It floors me today that naïve fans still buy into the notion that the steroids don't make you superhuman. The fact is that if they did not work, and did not work exceptionally well, players wouldn't risk their health to use them. Many players opted to use them.

Eric Newman was not one of them. He knew that using steroids was cheating and he just could not bring himself to cheat. He had that much integrity.

I wish this story ended with me writing that Eric Newman pitched in the Major League All Star Game without the use of steroids, but it does not end that way. It ends with Eric Newman retiring having never achieved his childhood dream of playing major league baseball.

It also ends with Eric Newman shining as an all-star example in life, something so much bigger than the game of baseball. To this day he has kept his integrity and never has to look at himself in the mirror as one who could get what he wanted only by cheating. Today he is married and a head collegiate baseball coach. He is a father, a husband, a mentor, a coach and a father figure to many, and they are fortunate to have a man with such integrity in that capacity.

Chapter 66

▲

STICKING WITH IT

ANTHONY CARUSO

"A diamond is a lump of coal that stuck with it."
    -Unknown

In youth sports, sometimes players are so evenly matched, coaches have a hard time choosing who should be the starter of the game and who should be on the bench. Such was the case with young Anthony Caruso, an aspiring goalie in ice hockey. Sometimes he would start, other times he would watch the entire game as a fellow teammate played in the goal.

Anthony caught a break on his thirteenth birthday, or so he thought. See, Anthony has an inordinate amount of passion for ice hockey. Honestly, it is quite fascinating. I have coached over 11,000 athletes and I am not sure I have seen it duplicated. He is watching, playing, coaching, teaching or talking ice hockey 24 hours a day as if nothing else in the world exists. In Anthony's world, nothing else does exist.

To Anthony's delight, he actually had a game scheduled on his thirteenth birthday. The coach announced him as the starter, in honor of his big day. What could be better for him—to get to play a game on his birthday, and to be the starting goalie? It would no doubt be a huge success for him.

There is no politically correct, soft or happy way to say this. Anthony played as badly as any athlete could possibly play that day. I know, I am supposed to be writing a happy story about a guy who had a shut-out that day, but the fact is Anthony Caruso gave up thirteen goals that day. Yes, he gave up thirteen goals on his thirteenth birthday. The team lost thirteen to nothing.

(Photo courtesy Rich Caruso).

Fortunately, the story does not end there. Through much work, hundreds of thousands of gallons of sweat shed, countless hours of film study, lack of sleep, supplemental off-ice strength and conditioning work-outs and giving virtually everything he had, Anthony again got to start on his birthday. This was now his fourteenth birthday and this time his team won 3-0. Yes, the guy who gave up thirteen goals on his thirteenth birthday stuck with it, and gave up no goals on his fourteenth.

Is there something in your life you need to just stick with in order to turn the horrible into the amazing?

Chapter 67

THE UGLY DUCKLING BECAME A SWAN
FRED ERICKSON

"Change always comes bearing gifts."
 -Price Pritchett

I hated him. There is no other way to say it. I sure dislike writing this since I wrote a chapter in my first book about not judging others and then followed that book with this one in which three separate chapters were dedicated towards having a proper perspective.

The fact is, Fred Erickson was hatable. He was in karate. He was big, strong, tough and mean. He also had some seriously ugly karate. I had seen a dozen guys like him the past—guys who did not have clean technique and struggled to win because they had a tough time technically. They all resort to pure unadulterated brutality. It's their means of finding a way to win when they cannot do so technically. I personally saw Fred do this to a few of my training partners – brutalize them physically – and I knew one day I would end up across the ring from him.

That day happened in a tournament in Fountain Hills, AZ in 2004. I committed to judge for several hours and to compete in the open black belt division against all of the young studs Arizona had to offer. The tournament was held shortly after I lost a dear friend to death: Pat Tillman. I was crushed. I am not ashamed to say I sat in that judge's chair for six hours that day with tears coming out of my eyes the entire time. It was a horrible thing for me to have to endure.

Up walks Fred as I am judging.

"There are no other guys in the 35+ age group and I want to compete. Would you fight me?"

I honestly wanted to hit him right there, grieving from the loss of Pat.

"No," I said, making sure I said it in a tone that left no room for changing my mind.

An hour later I fought in the 19-34 year old black belt division, with several national class young fighters. I fought Simeon Ekrisson, a multiple time national place-winner, who kicked me below the belt and received a point for it. I was on fire, not only had he kicked me illegally, but they also scored him a point. My butt was in mega-spasm and I was furious. I was left hurting and behind in points, not to mention the mood I was in, still grieving. I did the only thing I could do. I fired off the line in full intention and kicked him as hard as I could with my shin bone, right in his butt cheek, knowing full well it was illegal. It was an eye for an eye in my eyes. I didn't care: all I wanted to do was get him back. But there was a problem. When I kicked him as hard as I could, it wasn't with my shin bone. I missed and hit the top of my foot, hyperextending my ankle and tearing tendons. To top it all off, I got a formal reprimand from the same referee that gave Simeon a point for kicking me below the belt. I lost that match 2-1. I could not have been angrier: with myself, with Simeon, with the referee and about the loss of Pat.

"Hey Tim, please fight me, there aren't any others in my division," I heard with my back to Fred.

"No."

He then proceeded to try a third time, like I was going to change my mind.

I had had enough. I said yes. I did what I had to that day. I trashed him. I knew he was going to come at me with nothing but extreme force so I went at him with extreme force. I always win ugly fights.

That wasn't the end of Fred. I had to fight him about 15 more times in all of the local tournaments the following years. I beat him in all of them. He was my adversary. I had to dislike him, to villianize him. You never mind trashing a villain. Sometimes you feel bad about trashing a really good guy, so if he is a villain it makes life easier.

As fate would have it, we started talking more after each time we fought and I found him to be a truly nice person. I had to switch my thoughts from hating him all the time to hating him when we fought and liking him afterwards. I found myself teaching more often at his home dojo and I saw how hard he worked, how passionate he was about fighting and how good a person he was. Next I found myself traveling throughout the country with him to national level tournaments. I was having a great time with him, my newfound friend.

It has now been 9 years since we started traveling all over this country to compete and I see Fred in an entirely different light. He could not be a better guy, honestly. He is helpful, brilliant, super passionate about karate, fun to be around, helpful and someone I really enjoy spending time with. I would be remiss in not mentioning Fred's karate today. The years of hard work have really paid off. He has gotten very good technically, and earned the rank of third degree black belt. His fighting, even in his mid fifties, continues to get better each year. He has gone on to win National Championships in recent years against guys that used to beat him every year. In 2012, he also won the prestigious U.S. Open and we were all so happy for him, proud of him and thankful to see of the lesson he has taught us all. I also must be fair and mention he has ended my winning streak against him and has beaten me a couple of times.

The transformation reached its apex when I asked him to go to lunch last week. I wanted to pick his brain on his thoughts while fighting. It was fascinating for me to be in that role. Once upon a time he was a guy with ugly karate that I hated, now he is a cherished friend whom I lean on for help in my karate.

I would have never expected this story would end this way—Fred and I, close friends, with me asking him for advice to help my fighting. It sure beats the old days. Thank you Sir, for being the great guy you are, for helping me when I am in need, and for showing me how to keep progressing, even when others say you cannot. You now serve as a role model for me. Count me as your most respecting fan. I can pass no higher compliment than that.

Fred Erickson has shown me that ugly ducklings can indeed become swans, a lesson I hope to call upon in endeavors of my life where I am that ugly duckling.

The Fred I'm so glad I got to know.

Chapter 68

CONVICTION

BECKY

"Never, "for the sake of peace and quiet," deny your own experience or convictions."

    -Dag Hammarskjold

My meeting with Becky was purely by coincidence. I was at the 2012 Olympic Trials in wrestling. They were held at the Carver-Hawkeye Arena in Iowa City, Iowa, the University of Iowa's home gym. During a brief intermission I ran up to the bathroom.

It was during this dash that I noticed Ashley, Jon Reader's girlfriend. She cordially introduced me to Becky, who was decked out in very distinguishable Iowa State University gear. By all means, do not mistake the cardinal and gold of the Iowa State Cyclones with the black and gold of The University of Iowa Hawkeyes.

"It's nice to meet you Becky. I can guess who you are rooting for," I said.

"Yes, I am here for Jon and all of the Iowa State guys. It sure is tough for me to come here."

I wondered why it was tough for a diehard Cyclone to come root for other Cyclones, so I asked her why it was tough.

"I just don't want to be in THIS PLACE. I dislike the black and yellow so much. I love pepper and I love corn but I won't put the pepper on my corn."

Pepper on corn. If she likes pepper and likes corn, why doesn't she just put the pepper on the corn, I wondered.

Then it dawned on me: black and yellow cannot go together for a diehard Cyclone fan.

It was a thirty second meeting, I never even got her last name, but that is all it took for me to learn of true conviction.

Chapter 69

SEPARATION DOESN'T HAVE TO MEAN SEPARATION

MIKE LAMBERT

"It's not too late to develop new friendships or reconnect with people.."
    -Morrie Schwartz

If you have read thorough the chapters of this book and its predecessor, *Inner Strength Inner Peace*, you already know I was heavily involved in the sport of powerlifting in the 1980's. I competed as a lifter, coached the top drug-free lifters in the world, judged, ran contests and wrote several magazine articles. If it had to do with the squat, bench press or deadlift I was all over it. I left no stone unturned. I knew everyone in the sport and they knew me.

Mike Lambert, the face of powerlifting.
(Photo courtesy Mike Lambert.)

The nicest of all these people I was blessed to interact with was Mike Lambert. Mike owned and served then, as he still does now, as Editor and Publisher of *Powerlifting USA* magazine, undeniably the sports top magazine. I dealt with Mike quite a bit. I wrote seventeen articles for *Powerlifting USA*, ranging from secretive Bulgarian training principles to short leg syndrome to National Championships reporting. I also collaborated with him on the records established within the American Drug Free Powerlifting Association, as I was their records chairman, and he would publish the results. At times when he couldn't cover National meets, I would be entrusted to the reporting of results. Three times I hosted National Championships at Arizona State University and Mike came to cover them. Often times we would sit at the same meet, side by side, shooting pictures.

I'll never be as nice a guy as Mike Lambert was to me all those years. I wish I could be. I just must not have the genetic make-up to do so. To say he was nice is a huge disservice. He was well beyond nice. He was courteous, respectful and caring. He was fun and took time out of his days to educate me on photography and the history of powerlifting. He was one of those guys you knew was a much better guy than you are and you hoped he would be in your life forever.

That didn't happen. I got so busy at A.S.U. coaching 650 athletes a year I had no time left for my hobby of powerlifting. Mike and I were separated. It was that way for a good five years or so.

I hate to voluntarily divulge the following information, but one year I woke up on Christmas day around 2 a.m. with an entire article in my mind about how lifters could increase their total. I know, now I'm embarrassed. Other guys are dreaming about Carrie Underwood or being the next heavyweight champion of the world, and I'm dreaming of educating powerlifters on how to lift more. What can I say? I think I have an idiot savant, which is defined as "an intellectually disabled person who exhibits extraordinary ability in a highly specialized area, such as mathematics or music." Other guys get to do math and music. I get stuck seeing an entire years worth of detailed lifting programs in one picture in my mind. Sure, it has served me well. I have trained over 11,000 athletes and hundreds of elite professionals and I have never met one I could not quickly and significantly enhance, but I also sometimes wonder what I have accomplished if I put that brain power elsewhere.

At any rate, I called Mike out of the blue and was thrilled to reconnect. Better yet – he hadn't changed a bit. He was the same ole awesome Mike Lambert, the face of powerlifting. He was as giving and gracious as ever.

Fast forward was another decade. I finished *Inner Strength Inner Peace*, which contained several stories of powerlifters. Again I reconnected with Mike. I wanted to see about taking out an advertisement in *Powerlifting USA*. Again, he was there for me as if we had never had any time apart. He was the same guy again. I felt as though I was stepping back in decades gone by.

Mike Lambert owes me nothing, yet he gives so much to me unselfishly. He did in the 80's when I interacted with him frequently and he does to this day. The years, miles and career paths separated us, yet he always makes me feel like there was never any separation between us. Indeed, he is one of those special guys and one I hope to emulate some day.

Chapter 70

THE IMPORTANCE OF FORGIVENESS

KEVIN WYSSMANN

"To err is human, to forgive divine."
    -Alexander Pope

One brief look at Kevin Wyssmann and you are instantly drawn to him. He is an upbeat-looking, silver-haired gentleman whose appearance reflects peace, wisdom and contentment. His doctoral degree backs up the wisdom you can't help but notice when you see him. He has a soothing presence that attracts people to him. I was one of those people.

Dr. Wyssmann was teaching a class I attended. The subject of forgiveness was brought up. To illustrate the importance of forgiveness, Dr. Wyssmann brought up one of his own life stories.

When he was in eighth grade in a tiny Oklahoma town, he and a friend decided to pull a minor prank on a teacher to get a laugh out of their classmates. According to Kevin, one of his teachers was a small man and in order to get their laugh they yelled the words, "hey, Mighty Mouse," and "squeak, squeak," out the windows. The plan failed: the teacher didn't hear them. They had to repeat the procedure to get the rise out of their fellow students that they sought. This time they were successful, well, kind of successful. Indeed, their fellow students heard them, and so did the teacher, but he didn't laugh. He pulled out the paddle and got revenge. Over and over again. Kevin Wyssman was the recipient.

Kevin Wyssmann harbored a huge grudge against this teacher for about a decade. In the tiny community of Enid, Oklahoma, he ran into him constantly, in school, in church, in the town. He never spoke to him or acknowledged him. He merely hated him.

It was some time later when he was in a class himself that the subject of forgiveness was brought up and the students were told if they were harboring any resentments (even if they seemed justified) that they themselves were sinning, that unforgiven acts cause the resentful bearer to sin. Kevin Wyssmann knew what he had to do. He didn't want to bear the sin any longer. He had to drop the burden of his sin by asking the teacher for forgiveness for his disliking him for so many years.

When I heard this story, I was in a Bible study class at Christ's Greenfield Lutheran Church in Gilbert, Arizona. The class was taught by Rev. Dr. Kevin Wyssmann, the senior associate pastor. He asked us if we were harboring any long-term dislikes. I had one.

I had been a very innovative, successful strength and conditioning coach at Arizona State University. Our department there flourished. During my last year there, my evaluation by the assistant athletic director, my boss at the time, was off the charts. He could not have been more complimentary. He told me point blank everyone in the department loved my work. I thought I'd be there forever.

My contract was not renewed only a few months later. The cause was the football coach at the time, Bruce Snyder.

Bruce had just finished his third unsuccessful year at ASU after a very successful tenure at Cal. His staff came to ASU arrogant on their previous success and we all bought in to the thought that they would replicate it. They didn't. They lost and they lost often.

My final year there we entered the season with great hopes. In the preseason press conference Bruce Snyder emphatically stated, "This is the strongest, best conditioned team I have ever had." I was ecstatic.

That team went 3-8 and my contract was not renewed. I was bitter. I had built that department from the ground up and it was functioning exceptionally well. By Snyder's own admission and the athletic administration's, I had done an exceptional job, only to end up the scapegoat for others' failures. I was officially unemployed, divorced from a job I loved in a department I largely built. My contract was not renewed not because of the work I had done, but because of the work others did not do, winning football games. I harbored resentment.

I knew in hearing Pastor Wyssmann's talk I had to forgive Bruce Snyder, because not forgiving his action was causing me to be an unforgiving sinner. I didn't really expect it to happen though. Bruce was dying from cancer and the local newspapers reported he didn't have long to live.

Interestingly enough, as could only happen in my life, a few weeks later, a guy in the gym where I ran my business, came to me and told me Bruce Snyder was coming in that day, in case "I wanted to disappear for a few hours." He knew how I had previously felt about Bruce. I did not disappear that day. I did something much better. I forgave Bruce Snyder. I volunteered to help him if he needed me to. It was a far cry from my old fighting mentality of "God forgives, Tim McClellan doesn't." I was freed from the sin, thanks to my amazing pastor.

Bruce Snyder died a just few days later and Pastor Wyssmann has since taken a call to a church in Overland Park, Kansas. When you add up the events that had to take place to make all of this happen, it is literally mindboggling. I guess, with my hard head, it had to be a set of occurrences nothing short of miraculous to get through to me…but, then again, God does do miracles.

Pastor Wyssmann, thank you for changing my life, then and forever. I know you're doing the same for others. I pray you never stop.

▲ ABOUT THE AUTHOR

A self-described "ordinary guy with extraordinary determination," Tim McClellan, M.S., C.S.C.S. has distinguished himself worldwide during the past three decades as an innovator in the performance enhancement field. Among those he coached are more than 200 NFL players, 12 Olympic gold medalists, more than a dozen NCAA individual champions, 9 NCAA team champions, more than 200 NCAA All-Americans and National Champions of 17 different sports. Tim also coached at Arizona State University for 13 years and has worked with the USA Olympic wrestling team, the World Champion USA powerlifting team, and the Boston Bruins. The National Strength and Conditioning Association honored him in 1990 as a recipient of their President's Award.

A multiple National Champion himself in karate-do, Tim holds black belt ranks in five different martial arts. He has written numerous magazine articles, produced a variety of instructional videos and is the author of *Inner Strength Inner Peace*.

FINAL THOUGHTS

May you be thankful for the many blessings you receive from the great teachers around you and may you serve as one to others.

Tim McClellan

www.ingramcontent.com/pod-product-compliance
Lightning Source LLC
Chambersburg PA
CBHW080502110426
42742CB00017B/2969